*Music in the Moment*

# Music in the Moment

## JERROLD LEVINSON

*Cornell University Press*

ITHACA AND LONDON

First published 1997 by Cornell University Press.

Printed in the United States of America

Cornell University Press strives to utilize environmentally responsible suppliers
and materials to the fullest extent possible in the publishing of its books. Such
materials include vegetable-based, low-VOC inks and acid-free papers that are
also either recycled, totally chlorine-free, or partly composed of nonwood fibers.

*Library of Congress Cataloging-in-Publication Data*
Levinson, Jerrold.
    Music in the moment / Jerrold Levinson.
      p.  cm.
    ISBN 0-8014-3129-8 (cloth : alk. paper)
    1. Music—Philosophy and aesthetics.  2. Musical perception.
  3. Music—Psychology.  I. Title.
    ML3845.L47  1997
    781.1'7—dc21                97-19847

Cloth printing    10 9 8 7 6 5 4 3 2 1

*To Leonard and Geoffrey*

*Here will we sit, and let the sounds of music*
*Creep in our ears: soft stillness and the night*
*Become the touches of sweet harmony.*

—William Shakespeare, *The Merchant of Venice*

# CONTENTS

# MUSICAL ILLUSTRATIONS

# PREFACE

No doubt some people never heard much in music before they acquired conscious insight into its large-scale form. And surely there are others who, having acquired analytical dispositions and descriptive technical resources in the course of their musical education, found their fundamental listening transformed to a truly significant degree. But I am not one of them, and I suspect that such listeners are not the norm among those who can rightly claim both to know and to love the bulk of what constitutes the broad repertoire of classical music. It is an implicit aim of this book to defend such listeners—ones who, though untutored, are experienced, attentive, and passionate.

The primary and explicit aim of this book, however, is to combat the notion, often only implicit in the writing of many music commentators and theoreticians, that keeping music's form—in particular, large-scale structural relationships, or spatialized representations of a musical composition's shape—before the mind is somehow central to, even essential for, basic musical understanding. What I maintain instead is that much in the aural comprehension of extended pieces of music that seems to implicate explicit architectonic awareness can be explained by appeal to tacit, unconscious correlation of present passages or bits with earlier ones, rather than explicit, conscious grasp of relationships of a broad-span sort.

I wish to impugn, by consequence, the supposition that a listener must acquire formal or structural knowledge in an explicit manner to achieve musical comprehension, even of extended compositions.

It may be said that traditional formal analysis, aimed at delineating musical shape in the large, was always meant primarily as a description of the musical object, or perhaps of what comprehending listeners heard on a subconscious level, rather than being promoted as a requirement for or avenue to musical appreciation. Yet it has often seemed to take on that latter role in many people's minds, and in many writers' hands. This book is intended, in part, as antidote to that tendency to misapply the results of musical analysis.

Now it is a further and separate question to what extent a listener who has achieved basic aural comprehension of a piece of music, or who is musically literate in a tradition generally, possesses knowledge of musical structure in an articulate manner, rather than behaviorally or experientially. It is the question whether such knowledge must be verbally expressible, at least under guiding or prompting. I am inclined to think the answer is no. Even if the comprehending listener must have internalized, through repeated listening, certain facts of musical structuring in order to follow a piece aurally as he or she does, this does not entail that the listener has encoded such facts linguistically, or has access to such facts in a linguistic mode, even after careful eliciting. To think otherwise is to overlook the extent to which concepts can inform perception tacitly, and the extent to which understanding may be embodied in a set of dispositions to respond or discriminate or reproduce, rather than a set of abilities to categorize or label or describe. Thus what is, admittedly, a usual concomitant of achieved understanding is by some wrongly made into a necessary condition of its presence.

Of course one grasps the form of a piece of music, in some sense, as one listens to it comprehendingly, and doubtless representations of some sort enable that grasp to occur, but there is little reason to think those representations of musical formedness are essentially verbal, or even verbalizable, ones. Those who propose the ability to offer descriptions of music as prerequisite to basic musical understanding make two mistakes: first, the representations in terms of which music is grasped may not be articulate in nature; second, even if they were, being able to access them after listening so as to produce descriptions of the music would at most be evidential, but neither necessary nor sufficient, for having had a hearing experience of the right sort. The descriptivists concerning musical understanding confuse an ability commonly associated with comprehending listening—articulating in words what has been heard and responded to—with ones more nearly criterial of such listening.

The degree of linguistic expressibility of a listener's understanding of music is not, however, the main affair of this book, important as that issue is. The guiding concern is rather the degree to which such understanding requires reflective or intellectual awareness of musical architecture or large-scale musical structuring. Concatenationism, the view I derive from Edmund Gurney and, with qualifications, defend, says that that degree is approximately zero. All that basic understanding requires is, as it were, listening in the moment.

.   .   .

This book, though little, has been long in gestation. I have been mulling over the matters treated in it for more than fifteen years, and parts of the manuscript go back nearly as far. Whether it is a good thing I have at last decided to offer these observations and reflections in print will be for others to decide.

It is worth saying at the outset, though it will quickly be obvious, that this book is founded in the main on just one individual's listening experience of music—mine. I would probably never have had sufficient nerve to write about that experience, however, if I had not discovered in Edmund Gurney a kindred spirit of a century ago, and if I did not have the impression of a vast, silent legion of architectonically unconcerned music listeners for whom I hoped, in some part, to be speaking.

A different version of the first part of this book, roughly Chapters 1 through 3, appeared earlier as "Edmund Gurney and the Appreciation of Music," *Iyyun: The Jerusalem Philosophical Quarterly* 42 (1993): 181–205. I am grateful to Hebrew University, and especially Professor Eddy Zemach, for the opportunity to present these ideas publicly, in January 1992, at the Ninth Jerusalem Philosophical Encounter devoted to the philosophy of art.

I express special gratitude to the two readers of this book in manuscript, Douglas Dempster and Fred Maus, for providing many valuable suggestions, and for saving me from a number of errors. Doubtless many remain.

I am grateful also to Stephen Davies, Michael Slote, and most of all Georges Rey, who at different stages read complete drafts of the book and provided constructive criticism of it. That I did not take all their advice is my fault, not theirs. I thank also other friends and colleagues who influenced, through comments of one sort or another, the shape and content of this book: Mark DeBellis, Stan Godlovitch, Ruth Hacohen, Daniel Herwitz, Monique Roelofs, Roger Scruton, Kim Sterelny, and Kendall Walton.

I thank the General Research Board of the University of Maryland for research leave during the Spring 1996 semester, a part of which was spent revising the manuscript of this book.

I thank once again Roger Haydon and the staff at Cornell University Press for the high level of support they have accorded me, as well as for the confidence they have shown in my work. Finally, I thank my brother, Leonard Levinson, and my cousin, Geoffrey Argent, my earliest companions in listening, who were there when the world of music first opened up for me, and when the ideas about its appreciation defended in this book were most likely already taking root.

JERROLD LEVINSON

*College Park, Maryland*

*M u s i c   i n   t h e   M o m e n t*

*c   h   a   p   t   e   r      o   n   e*

# EDMUND GURNEY AND THE
# EXPERIENCE OF MUSIC

A creature cannot be beautiful if it is too great, for contemplation of
it cannot be a single experience, and it is not possible to derive a sense
of unity and wholeness from our perception of it.

—Aristotle, *Poetics*

Edmund Gurney was an English psychologist and musician who
lived from 1847 to 1888. His major work, *The Power of Sound* (1880),
is a vast treatise on musical aesthetics, ranging from issues in acoustics
to the question of the origin of music and the relation of music to
morality. It is doubtless the most important work of its kind in the latter
half of the nineteenth century, though it has not received attention
commensurate with its stature. Commentators often lump Gurney together with Eduard Hanslick as a musical formalist, but his view on the
expressive dimension of music is neither as restrictive nor as doctrinaire
as Hanslick's. Hanslick insists on denying to music specific emotional
content, though he allows it to convey general dynamic features which
emotions, among other things, exhibit. Gurney, on the other hand, allows
that some music possesses fairly definite emotional expression. What he
is primarily concerned to deny is that musical beauty or impressiveness
is either the same as, or depends on, definiteness of expression of emotion.

I am not here concerned with Gurney's views on musical expression,
interesting as they are.[1] I want to focus on Gurney's conception of the

1. For discussion, see Malcolm Budd, *Music and the Emotions,* chap. 4, and my "Gurney, Edmund."

music listening experience itself. Gurney has fairly controversial ideas
concerning the workings and limits of musical apprehension, and the
consequences he draws for the nature of musical form, the basis of musical
enjoyment, and the grounds of musical evaluation are striking indeed.
Among other things, there is implicit in Gurney's view an important
challenge to the relevance that musical analysis, that is, analysis of large-
scale structure, can have for musical appreciation, or the understanding
of music as heard. This challenge needs to be carefully assessed.

Basically, Gurney maintains that *large-scale form in music is, at most,
of minor relevance to the appreciation and evaluation of music.* The important thing in musical comprehension, he holds, is the grasping of individual parts as they occur, and the grasping of connections to immediately
neighboring parts fore and aft. The value of a piece, furthermore, is solely
a function of the satisfyingness, to the purely intuitive musical faculty,
of its individual bits and the cogency of sequence exhibited at transitions
between bits. Gurney's view thus emphasizes the concrete detail of musical surface and its quality and connectedness from moment to moment
almost to the exclusion of any other factor one might think relevant to
the experience of music.

This outlook on music is clearly inimical to one many music theorists
and educators seem to adopt implicitly—namely, that the elucidation
and awareness of large-scale structural relations is of great and primary
relevance to the understanding of musical works, and that the whole is
indeed as important as the parts, if not more so. It seems to me, however,
that Gurney's outlook is in fact the sounder of the two. The simple
insight at the heart of Gurney's position is one I believe to be valid, and
one that promoters of overall form tend to forget. It is that music of
any extent consists of a series of successive events, which cannot be
apprehended simultaneously in a single perceptual act. The parts of an
architectural facade can be taken in more or less in one sweep; the parts
of a symphony cannot. Of course the earlier portions of a musical work
can be revisited in memory as listening proceeds, or the later portions
entertained in anticipation—though neither without cost to absorption
in the music at hand—but doing so does not amount to having perceptual
experience of a whole. What is crucial, according to Gurney, is involvement in the musical progression from point to point, the local movement
from note to note and phrase to phrase. The essential form of music is

located there, he would claim, and not in architectonic vistas beyond the scope of aural experience.

.     .     .

My main concern in this book is the nature of the understanding that is at the core of a listener's experience of ordinary tonal music. This concern is linked up with two fundamental questions for which I hope to provide something of an answer: What is and is not crucial to musical comprehension on a listener's part? What are and are not primary grounds of value in music from a listener's point of view?

My initial approach to these questions will be by way of Gurney's views on musical experience. After exposition of Gurney's position I extract certain claims that typify the Gurneyan perspective on musical understanding. That perspective, which I refer to as *concatenationism,* becomes the focus of inquiry for the rest of this book. Essentially, I want to see how far one can defend concatenationism as an account of what is central and distinctive in the apprehension of music.

After explaining concatenationism and highlighting its prima facie plausibility, I review a number of considerations that militate against a strict concatenationist position. I then ask, in each case, what modifications or qualifications of concatenationism, if any, are in order in light of those considerations. Toward the end of the book I explore the implications of a concatenationist view of musical apprehension for the evaluation of musical works, for the notion of goodness of form in music, and for the degree of real kinship between music and those other arts usually denominated "temporal," the narrative arts of literature and film.

### Gurney on Form, Understanding, and Value in Music

A cornerstone of Gurney's view of music is the contrast he repeatedly draws between the temporal art of music and static two-dimensional visual art. Gurney is forcibly struck by the difference between the apprehension of music and the apprehension of a linear arabesque or architectural facade. Whereas one can have a single sweeping perception of the whole of an arabesque or facade, with music one can have only a series of perceptions of the parts of a work as it unfolds in time, but never a single perception of the work in its entirety. The experience of music is fundamentally a matter of individual momentary impressions.[2]

> In a melodic form there is no multiplicity or thronging of elements, no impression of conspiring parts all there at once. The elements are units succeeding one another in time; and though each in turn, by being definitely related to its neighbors, is felt as belonging to a larger whole, there is no simultaneity of impression. (92)

Despite the successiveness of our apprehension of them, however, the momentary parts of music regularly group themselves into extended units that we seem to grasp as a whole, though we cannot literally perceive them at one time. We find that some sequences of minute heard events cohere together strongly as they are sequentially perceived, so that we hear them as single unified motions. This is the phenomenon of *melody:* a string of successive auditory impressions somehow adding up to a single impression comprising them all. The most important criterion of melody for Gurney is that it be a sequence of notes that together have a certain minimum "rightness." This rightness can be understood, it seems, counterfactually, in terms of the effects that changing single notes would bring about. It is

> a general feature of melodies, good, bad, and indifferent. What is meant is that each unit falls definitely in its right place as an obviously essential part of the whole such as it is; strike out or alter a note here or there, and what was an organic whole is either broken into more or less incoherent fragments; or if in some exceptional instance it retains a satisfactory coherence, it is by becoming something else, recognized as another whole. If less marked notes are selected for omission, the melody may indeed retain a coherence as a ghost of its former self; but it would usually fail to give a notion of its true self to a person who heard it first in the mutilated form. (92–93)

2. All page references in parentheses are to Edmund Gurney, *Power of Sound*. The reader should bear in mind the period of music that Gurney has reference to for his reflections on music, which is roughly that of Bach to Wagner.

The special quality or character of a given melody is dependent on every note it comprises; change any one and invariably the result will be either no melody or new melody. Any true conception of the form of a melody requires apprehending each and every element for what it is as it occurs. By contrast, the general outline or contour of a melody gives practically no idea of the melody whatsoever. The essence of a melody lies in the specific notes that go to make it up, and not in anything more general that may be abstracted from them.[3]

Gurney later supplements this counterfactual criterion of melody with one more directly phenomenological. It is a mark of a melody that one is familiar with that when one is strictly hearing only one part of it, it is *as if* one were hearing the whole thing at each moment as well. One is in some way aware of the remainder while hearing any one part.

> When a melody is familiar to us we realize it by a gradual process of advance along it, while yet the *whole* process is in some real manner present to us at each of the successive instants at which only a minute part of it is actually engaging our ears. (165)

Gurney observes that once a melody is known, the opening bars seem to convey in prospect all the beauty of the rest, which evidences the hearer's grasp of a whole present in each of its parts. Gurney also notes another related feature of a melody which one has gotten to know—that in listening to it one seems to evolve it from within oneself, one seems to construct the melody, with its characteristic tensions and overall flavor, by the very act of listening. This is all a consequence of the ear's unique "faculty of linking a long series of swiftly vanishing impressions into a unity" (174).[4]

---

3. For Gurney, pitch and rhythm are equally important and thoroughly interdependent components of melody. So by "change of note" one is to understand a change in either pitch or rhythm.

4. Readers familiar with *Power of Sound* will note the omission in this discussion of Gurney's notion of "ideal motion." In my view, Gurney's exposition of that notion is unhelpfully unclear. It is hard to say, for one thing, if ideal motion is a quality of musical forms as heard or of the psychological processes responsible for such hearing. I believe that everything important in Gurney's view on the essential nature of melody can be explained without entering into exactly what Gurney had in mind by "ideal motion."

The emergence of melody, whether supported harmonically or not, is thus the chief way in which the fundamental moment-to-moment nature of musical apprehension is tempered and, to an extent, transcended. Gurney is willing, however, to admit the existence of larger unities, for instance, musical paragraphs, provided the components of such are bound together in a certain way. Although such paragraphs, unlike melodies, are not experienced as wholes, they can be internally unified so that their successive parts do not strike a listener as independent, self-contained, and without connection to one another.

What is required for this impression of connectedness is called by Gurney *organicity* or *cogency of sequence*. It would be fair to say that cogency of sequence, for Gurney, is the one and only criterion of effective musical form. It is the sine qua non of well-formedness at any level; it is possessed by the succession of unprepossessing two- and three-note fragments that make up a melody, and it is possessed by the succession of melodic and transitional passages that make up a unified musical paragraph. In the first case, one has parts (the individual tones) that are not themselves impressive combined into a unit that is, whereas in the second case, the parts are already independently impressive, though they yield a whole that is impressive as well. In discussing what it is for a musical paragraph to constitute a form in the strict sense, Gurney offers this characterization of cogency of sequence, in which its application to melody as well is plain:

A paragraph, if it is to be musically valuable, cannot arrive at any great length without being provided with some clear principle of unity; for example, the frequent reiteration of a recognizable phrase, as in the development of a subject, or in the persistence of a certain kind of figure or rhythmic group. A long succession of phrases which exhibits nothing but perpetual differentiation will escape the grasp of the ear, and will seem rambling and aimless. *But whether or not united in some such special manner, any paragraph which is to be musically valuable must satisfy the test that each bit shall necessitate, as it were, and so enter into organic union with the one next to it:* Nor, indeed, is the application of such a test confined to long paragraphs: we can divide a more compact passage . . . into subordinate groups of notes; and in proportion as we feel nothing cogent in their union, and could

hear changes and substitutions in them with indifference, is the series one which fails to give us the characteristic delight of a melodic
form. . . . The cardinal idea of organic form in any musical sentence
or paragraph is . . . *cogency of sequence at each point:* a long series of
periods may exhibit it throughout, and the shortest fragment may lack
it. (204; my emphases)

Cogency of sequence, then, is each part—whether motive, phrase,
melody, or paragraph—leading convincingly to the next, each consequent
appearing, upon familiarity, to be the natural, even inevitable continuation of each antecedent. Where there is cogency of sequence there is
resistance to any imagined substitution for any part in the musical chain.
The test of cogency is precisely "the feeling of resentment . . . with
which the ear, after sufficient acquaintance, would receive changes or
omissions" (212).

Cogency or organicity admits of degrees, however. It reaches its apex
within single melodies, tying together component motives or phrases. It
can run fairly high in a paragraph composed of several melodies and
quasi-melodic passages, and only a little less so in a section comprising
a few paragraphs. Degree of organicity is usually on the wane within
movements made up of several sections, and generally reaches the vanishing point with whole works containing a number of movements. These
are generalizations, of course; much depends on the particular sorts of
melody, of movement, of work involved. Gurney recognizes, for example,
that a movement in ABA form standardly displays less cogency of sequence between its sections than a movement in sonata form. They are
exemplars, respectively, of "two plans under which musical forms can be
put together; that of quasi-independent and serial juxtaposition, and that
where different sections are distinctly connected by the possession of
recognizable common features." Gurney elaborates further:

mere considerations of extent have very little to do with organic unity.
Quite short paragraphs in juxtaposition may have so little vital connection that one of them ought to be easily replaced by a kindred paragraph
out of some similar work . . . as might be exemplified very often in
the case of minuets and trios, and in the paragraphs of dances; while

much longer movements may be in a true sense organic through-out. (205)

One marked manifestation of the supreme organic coherence that a melody or musical paragraph can have for us is the phenomenon of recalling a bit from out of the middle of such a melody or paragraph and feeling distinctly that it is a part of a larger whole. One has a consciousness of the remainder of that whole, even though one cannot inwardly repro-duce it. The bit is recollected, in other words, not as an independently experienced, self-contained unit, but as a fragment, with a surrounding context, though this context is hidden, as it were, behind a veil.

Although there are in musical discourse "all degrees of closeness and laxness in the unifying bond" (206)—that is, though there is a continuum between the intimate union of phrases in a Mozart melody and the chockablock juxtaposition of large sections in some of Bruckner's fina-les—Gurney claims that in practice the middle degrees tend to go unin-stantiated, and so in many pieces we readily distinguish between formed units, which have a certain integrity and independent value, and mere arrangements of formed units, which do not evince any overarching unity of their own. There remains a distinction in kind, for Gurney, between stretches of music (e.g., melodies) whose component parts exhibit an "absolute indispensableness and interdependence" (212) and stretches of music (e.g., most sections, movements, and complete works) whose component parts fail to do so.

It is to be emphasized that for Gurney cogency of sequence—including unity of melody, which is a species of it—is a purely *intuitive* matter, judged by an autonomous musical faculty. It cannot be assessed or dem-onstrated by rational means; no formulable rules of repetition, contrast, balance, or the like can guarantee the presence of cogency or organic union. For Gurney the musical faculty, in accord with the phenomenolog-ical criteria which have been mentioned, is the ultimate arbiter of musical form or effectiveness.

I now return to the point with which our survey of Gurney's view began—the essential sequentialness of musical apprehension, and our inability to take in an extended portion of music as a whole at one stroke. Gurney insists that this basic fact entails the absolute primacy of the parts of a musical composition with regard to musical form, musical enjoyment, and musical worth. The *real* form of a piece of music is in effect exhausted by the constitution of the smallest independent units, that is, phrases and melodies, out of formless elements, and the specific manner in which each independent unit leads to the next. There is in no important sense an overall form to an extended piece of music; there is only formedness or cogency within and between bits that are successively apprehended. If the parts of a composition are each effective and fitting as they come, then there is little more to be desired in the way of form. Musical enjoyment, likewise, is grounded entirely in the grasp of individual bits of various sizes and transitions between them. And, ultimately, a musical work is worth only as much as its parts and the links connecting them. "The whole is a combination of parts successively enjoyed, and can only be impressive so far as the parts are impressive" (97). The parts, even taken by themselves out of context, are often of exceptional value; the whole comprising all the parts in order, however, carries no additional value of its own, beyond that attaching to the parts as successively encountered, arranged just as they are. As for relations that a given part may bear to other parts distant from it, these may indeed affect one's experience of the given part, but a listener's attention remains properly fixed on the part being heard, and not on any skein of relations encompassing the piece as a whole, in which the part may abstractly figure. Although awareness of some relation may enhance one's pleasure in what is then being heard, there is no distinct pleasure in the relation itself. The following is probably Gurney's most important statement of this crucial point:

> . . . the all-importance of the parts in a musical composition . . . is not contradicted by our recent discussion of the extension of organic unity into a large movement. . . . It is characteristic of the whole apprehension of Music, of all grades of perception of it from the highest to the lowest, that the attention is focussed on each part as it comes; and that we never get our impressions of a long musical movement, as we commonly do those of a great architectural structure, through views which sweep over and embrace the whole rather than dwell on the parts. Even though one part of a movement may owe its point in great measure to another, either through a contrast involving some faint sort of ideal representation of the other, or through

actual similarity and reference to the other, that definite relation is at most to another *part*, not to the whole, and its effect is to increase our pleasure *at a part*. The whole may be, or may become through familiarity, so truly organic as to make each part seem an unalterable phase of the continuous motion; but for all that it is in our enjoyment of the parts, one after another, that the quality of close and vital organism takes effect; the subtle relationship of part B to part A being one of the qualities of part B which makes the moments it occupies peculiarly delightful. Thus pleasure in the whole has no meaning except as expressing the sum of our enjoyments from moment to moment; a sum which will be increased in proportion as the organic principle pervades the whole. In fact, to say that the parts are all-important is merely to assert our inability to do what involves a contradiction in terms—to enjoy something the esence of which is a *succession* of impressions by a *simultaneous* review of all the impressions. (213–15)

An additional quotation concerning the listening relevance of extended relations and overall structure will not be out of place, in light of the importance this issue will assume in subsequent discussion:

. . . though it is true that when a subject is variously treated and developed, the enjoyment of the resulting members of the composition involves the recognition of the subject, and is to this extent dependent on what has gone before, this sort of retrospective and sequential relationship is clearly something different from the conspiring of mutually controlled parts to a single large effect. While our knowledge of the subject enters essentially into our appreciation of the various uses of it, at each fresh use our hearing is concentrated on the special bit of form then and there passing; and the relationship implied in recognition of our old acquaintance under a new aspect, though of the closest sort, is still between two parts . . . not between a whole multitude of parts, as in an elaborate building. (98)

Gurney believes that our central involvement with the successive parts that come our way one after another, and not with the totality that they constitute, is too often ignored by those who would pronounce on the essential beauty of musical works. He expends a good deal of energy berating theorists who emphasize the "architectonic" aspect in music, who wax rhapsodic about symmetries, ratios, proportions, and parallelisms, as if therein lay whatever worth a piece of music possessed. Such writers falsely imply

> the existence of some grand primary scheme, filled in with detail in the process of production, and capable now of being abstracted and admired apart from the actual bits of form which moment after moment engross the ear. . . . In music the notion of a larger and more essential design, in reference to which shorter individual strains are details in the sense of being less essential, has no application. *The scheme has no value apart from the bits.*[5] (215–16; my emphasis)

In sum, rationally justifiable features of large-scale organization have no direct relevance to either the appreciation or the evaluation of a piece of music. It is in the musical progression from point to point that a piece lives, and the quality of that progression is the principal criterion of its worth as music.

Finally, we may note that Gurney distinguishes between two modes of music listening, the *definite* and the *indefinite*. His conclusions concerning musical form, enjoyment, and value all presuppose and relate to listening occurring in the definite mode. Someone listening definitely attends to the specific features of the melodic and harmonic motion of the music as it passes, registers the individuality of what he hears, and has some recognition or recollection capacity for those bits of form as a result. Definite listening is active, alert, particularizing, and participatory. Someone listening indefinitely, on the other hand, is aware only of "successions of agreeably-toned and harmonious sounds" (306), and reacts to and registers only gross changes in the overall sound image. The definite listener takes pleasure in the details of musical motion at each point, whereas the indefinite listener takes pleasure in volume level, timbral variety, or richness of harmony for their own sakes. In a passage that recalls John Stuart Mill's well-known discussion of higher and lower

---

5. The sentence italicized would serve nicely as a slogan against the excesses of unbridled architectonicism—such as that implicit in, or at least inspired by, the theories of Heinrich Schenker.

pleasures in his *Utilitarianism,* Gurney asserts that the superiority of definite over indefinite listening is properly attested to precisely by those who have, at different times, experienced both. And in that we are happy to concur. But we shall not, in any case, be further concerned in this book with indefinite listening.

# STATEMENT AND ELABORATION
# OF CONCATENATIONISM

. . . all music must be followed phrase by phrase as a process in time.
—Donald Francis Tovey, *Essays in Musical Analysis*

I now extract from this review of Gurney four claims that epitomize the sort of position he holds, and which I will henceforth refer to as *concatenationism*. I choose this name because it expresses the idea that music essentially presents itself for understanding as a chain of overlapping and mutually involving parts of small extent, rather than either a seamless totality or an architectural arrangement. With only a little pressing, then, we may arrive at four propositions, concerned respectively with musical understanding, enjoyment, form, and value, whose conjunction constitutes concatenationism:

1. *Musical understanding* centrally involves neither aural grasp of a large span of music as a whole, nor intellectual grasp of large-scale connections between parts; understanding music is centrally a matter of apprehending individual bits of music and immediate progressions from bit to bit.[1]

---

1. This is a good place to note, before getting further under way, that by terms such as "intellectual grasp," "intellectual apprehension," "reflective awareness," and "contemplative grasp" in connection with music—terms to which I will often have recourse in order to express the foil to more basic aural involvement with music—I generally mean some *conscious cognition or thought*, involving representation of an articulate, spatial, or pictorial sort. But such cognitions or thoughts need be neither elaborate nor sustained; the threshold of "intellectual," "reflective," and "contemplative", in other words, is rather low.

2. *Musical enjoyment* is had only in the successive parts of a piece of music, and not in the whole as such, or in relationships of parts widely separated in time.

3. *Musical form* is centrally a matter of cogency of succession, moment to moment and part to part.

4. *Musical value* rests wholly on the impressiveness of individual parts and the cogency of the successions between them, and not on features of large-scale form per se; the worthwhileness of experience of music relates directly only to the former.

Concatenationism as so formulated is perhaps a bit stronger—more black-and-white—than the view actually held by Gurney. Its starkness, however, should facilitate discussion of its merits and demerits in the remainder of this book. Certainly concatenationism, on my construction of it, can be held to fairly represent the thrust of Gurney's thinking on the experience of music.

### Quasi-Hearing

Before considering the defensibility of such claims, I wish to bring out more clearly what I believe underpins them. On first glance, it may seem as if Gurney's rather startling views proceed directly from the simple observation that at any moment one is strictly hearing only one moment's worth of music. It might appear that Gurney is arguing from this proposition straightaway to the conclusion that for a listener, a piece can be no more than a series of discrete momentary impressions, thus obviously rendering irrelevant anything concerning the piece as a whole. But that would be a misreading, if not always of the text, then of the spirit of what Gurney is after.

For Gurney clearly has a somewhat broader conception of musical experience than the succession-of-independent-instants model. This conception is readily apparent in his discussion of melody. When one hears a familiar melody, a directed tonal movement, with comprehension one does not just aurally register each note in the fraction of a second it takes to present itself, one in some sense "hears" the whole at any point; that is, one has an aural grasp on an entity spread out in time, and thus not strictly present to the ear in its entirety at any moment.

Hearing musical movement is necessarily hearing a sonic entity not all of which is sounding at any instant, while at any instant, one hears the sounding notes as belonging to a musical flow, or as contained within a musical process, of which they form a part.[2] No conscious effort is required to keep music that has just sounded, or is about to sound, before the mind; rather, an aural surrounding to the notes then sounding constitutes itself automatically, for a prepared listener. It is useful to have a term for this sort of vivid apprehension of a musical unit, which goes beyond what is strictly heard, but stops well short of merely intellectual contemplation of a recollected event. An appropriate term for this sort of perceptual experience, I suggest, is "quasi-hearing."[3]

We might then say that although one literally *hears* only an instant of music at a time, one generally *quasi-hears,* or vividly apprehends, a somewhat greater extent of musical material. Paradigmatically, this apprehension occurs throughout the hearing of a melodic passage, but it may also occur at points of transition between two such cogently related passages. In any case, an important point is that the scope of quasi-hearing, of grasping a musical motion in one go—of seeming to hear a span of music while strictly hearing, or aurally registering, just one element of it—is generally fairly *small.* While clearly much greater than the twentieth of a second that constitutes what has been called the musical present,[4]

---

2. On the hearing of musical movement, see Hanslick, *The Beautiful in Music;* Langer, *Feeling and Form;* Zuckerkandl, *Sound and Symbol;* and Scruton, "Understanding Music." In a more deflationary mode, see Budd, "Understanding Music," and Stephen Davies, *Musical Meaning and Expression,* chap. 5.

3. I stress that, for better or worse, the idea of quasi-hearing is my own, not Gurney's. It is introduced in a spirit of rational reconstruction of the basis of Gurney's views on music, but also in the hope of capturing something true about the phenomenology of music listening. I note that roughly the same idea, though of course not labeled quasi-hearing, is expressed in a current psychology textbook: "We hear a melody and seem to perceive much or all of it in the present, even though the first chord has already ebbed away by the time the last note of the musical phrase reaches our ears" (Henry Gleitman, *Psychology,* p. 225).

4. Roughly, the shortest period of time in which the musically relevant features of a sound can be registered. See, on this, J. B. Davies, *Psychology of Music,* chap. 3. Bare capacity to discriminate two sound events, of course, goes much further down, perhaps to 1/200 of a second, as studies using clicks separated by ever smaller intervals of silence have demonstrated.

it rarely exceeds a minute or so in length, the actual duration depending on the nature of the musical material involved and the quality of its internal connectedness.

The experience of quasi-hearing can be usefully thought of as having three components or aspects. The first would be the *actual hearing* of an instant of music, the second would be the *vivid remembering* of a stretch of music just heard, and the third would be the *vivid anticipation* of a stretch to come. Vivid memory and vivid anticipation might be thought to provide tonal images that exist for listening consciousness simultaneously, yet somehow noninterferingly, with the current sound impression, in something like the way the peripheral objects of vision are present to the eye, though obliquely, at the same time as the object that is in central focus.[5] The width of the window of quasi-hearing, so conceived, is thus at any point a direct function of the reach of vivid memory and vivid anticipation at that point, which is a matter of the extent of virtual imaging backwards and forwards that the musical material and one's familiarity with it allow.[6]

5. Some have found the role of memory and anticipation in constituting melodies as heard so puzzling that they have been inclined to deny them any role at all: "let anyone who is capable of it call to mind the immediately preceding tone of a melody that he is hearing. *The instant he does so, he will have lost the thread of the melody.* The hearing of a melody is a hearing *with* the melody, that is, in closest connection with the tone sounding at the moment. It is even a condition of hearing melody that the tone present at the moment should fill consciousness *entirely,* that *nothing* should be remembered . . . any turning back of consciousness for the purpose of making past tones present immediately annuls the possibility of musical hearing" (Victor Zuckerkandl, *Sound and Symbol,* p. 231).

It is clear that Zuckerkandl here understands remembering only as the active bringing of some past event to the forefront of consciousness. But on less deliberate and intrusive construals of remembering, the consequences Zuckerkandl draws for the disruption of melody processing may not follow. (Zuckerkandl's alternative proposal, offered in the remainder of his text, is unfortunately the semimystical idea that in grasping melody what we essentially apprehend is pure futurity or temporal becoming.)

6. Probably the quality of imaging occurring in respect of tones already heard is different from and more substantial than, that occurring in respect of tones not yet heard. The images involved may be related to what psychologists have called mental echoes, the contents of auditory registers that hold information for a second or two after stimulus reception, as well as a product of the functioning of short-term memory proper, the extent of which for heard material appears to be on the order of five to fifteen seconds. See Henry Gleitman, *Psychology,* chap. 7.

Finally, it is possible that this account, in terms of faint tonal images, could ultimately be replaced by a more cautious one phrased in terms of strong dispositions to recall or project. But I think the supposition of such images in listening, however difficult they are to describe, is experientially warranted.

The span that one can quasi-hear at any time—how much one can have aurally almost-present to one—appears to be rather limited. It is to be measured in seconds or possibly minutes, not in hours or quarter-hours. Typically it extends no further than a single long melody. This last observation in fact suggests a convenient, if rough, criterion of the special kind of vivid aural grasp that I have labelled quasi-hearing: a span of music is being quasi-heard when it is being experienced by a listener as throughout having something approximating the degree of presentness, wholeness, and immediacy that a phrase, melody, or melodic passage possesses when heard with comprehension.[7]

I think one cannot adequately explain Gurney's account of musical experience without appealing to something like the notion of quasi-hearing. For Gurney, a listener who strictly only heard individual bits sequentially, without quasi-hearing any groups of them to form melodies or passages, could not be understanding the music—and not, note, because he was failing to grasp its large-scale shape, but rather because he was excluded from any sense of that cogency which Gurney regards as the sine qua non of music that is minimally successful; that is, that can be counted as music at all.[8]

One reason it is difficult to describe the experience of quasi-hearing, of knitting music into a whole over some short span, is that to do so one must, at least partially, leave that consciousness and adopt another that tries, so to speak, to catch it in the act. This second, observing consciousness, as Jean-Paul Sartre illuminatingly showed,[9] is a reflexive

7. Thomas Clifton's *Music as Heard*, chap. 3, contains an extended discussion of Husserl on the phenomenology of music listening. Husserl, in his *Phenomenology of Internal Time-Consciousness* (1925), spoke of the horizon of listening, of retention, of protention, and of a musical "now." Much of my account of Gurney on the apprehension of music could be stated in the above terms. For example, there are these rough parallels: retention—vivid memory; protention—vivid anticipation; the "now"—a quasi-hearable span surrounding a given instant; listening horizon—an extent of music beyond what is quasi-heard and providing a sort of context to that which is. My attention was drawn to Husserl's scheme by Clifton's book only after I had begun to formulate the basis of Gurney's position using my own notions. The two frameworks seem roughly isomorphic, with the possible exception of the marking of the quasi-hearing experience per se.
8. I should emphasize that in foregrounding melody, comprising both pitch movement and rhythmic pattern, in this discussion of the phenomenon of quasi-hearing, I do not mean to be slighting harmony as a unifying or cohering force in music as heard. A chord progression or a chain of suspensions might in principle have the same perceptual unity or aural wholeness as an accompanied or unaccompanied melody.
9. See Sartre, *L'Imaginaire*, chap. 1, sec. 3.

one, and different in character from the nonreflexive one that it aims to capture or observe. The problem is that in reflecting on this nonreflexive aural synthesis, we run the danger of transforming it into something else—something it becomes when it is introspected, rather than what it is when it is going on unselfconsciously and unmonitored. Since the target psychological process is, let us say, not a reflective one, while the examining one is explicitly so, we may worry that the examining consciousness may import some reflectiveness into its target that is not properly there. Recalling an earlier patch of listening experience, now completed, rather than focusing on one occurring in the present, provides a partial check against this kind of introspective corruption, but its deliverance is similarly subject to doubt, in addition to being temporally at a remove from the object of interest. The most we can do is to bear this difficulty in mind in trying to describe correctly the experience of comprehending listening.[10]

Quasi-hearing can be conceived as a process in which conscious attention is carried to a small stretch of music surrounding the present moment, and which involves synthesizing the events of such a stretch into a coherent flow, insofar as possible. None of that, however, entails that one is consciously *aware* of quasi-hearing—that is, of attending and synthesizing—while one is doing so, or conscious *that* one is consciously aware of only a small extent of music surrounding the presently sounding event. One is only so conscious, it seems, when deliberately out to observe or reflect on what one is tacitly doing, or to assess how far one's awareness of an ongoing piece is carrying. As already noted, the deliverances of consciousness on such occasions are inherently subject to doubt, but I think there is little else to rely on in this domain. In any event, I have relied on them, and will continue to do so, albeit circumspectly.

. . .

Gurney's general position might best be viewed as falling between these two truisms, and as trying to mediate between them: (1) one cannot *hear* more than a tiny bit, for example, half a measure, of music at one time, and (2) one can *contemplate* the whole of a piece of music, in some sense, by representing it in linear fashion in one's imagination. What

10. My suspicion, for what it is worth, is that it is precisely those who overintellectualize the experience in question who have fallen afoul of this difficulty.

Gurney is aiming at, by contrast, is this not-so-obvious intermediary observation: (3) one cannot have *quasi-hearing* experience of music— that is, a high degree of vivid apprehension, as exemplified in hearing a sequence of tones as a melody—for more than a minute or so, running at most, perhaps, to a paragraph composed of a few unusually integrated melodic passages. This appreciatively important span of quasi-hearing, or aural cogency, is clearly greater than the span of present hearing, which is strictly speaking an instant, but also clearly much shorter than the span of recollective contemplation, which is perhaps an entire movement or symphony.

Gurney is concerned to emphasize that the experience of envisaging a piece as a whole, when it has been retained in memory, is really nothing like the experience of music as heard, as registered and responded to in real time. In particular, it does not constitute a sort of higher hearing, nor any kind of compressed analog of the original experience. This contrast is a consequence of the fact that such envisaging consists, if anything, in an act of all-encompassing apprehension. But such global, instantaneous apprehension of a piece cannot involve sound images of individual parts, given that those images require time to run through or traverse; a fortiori, it cannot be construed as a succession of such runnings-through, from beginning to end. The implication, for Gurney, is clear; architectonic contemplation of musical structure, whenever it might occur, is an experience of music in quite a different, and rather more etiolated, sense than that involved in a listener's active weaving together of the strands of a musical fabric when quasi-hearing its moment-by-moment progression. The distance, for Gurney, between large-scale structural contemplation and quasi-hearing of a melodic passage of several measures is greater than that between this latter and literal hearing of some present note, interval, or cadence. There is a difference of kind, not just one of degree, between quasi-hearing a stretch of music and cognizing the overarching form of a musical composition of some extent, a difference that is phenomenologically marked.

Another way to come to Gurney's point is through a contrast of music with painting. If one tries to achieve an overall grasp of a painting, the parts that need to be related and integrated into a total sign, as it were, are all of them perceptually present, accessible to visual contemplation of a sustained sort. But with a musical composition of any extent the parts that call for such relation and integration are most of them perceptually absent, and representable only through memories, whether of a verbal or nonverbal type. Thus, it seems that one cannot *perceive* the form of such a musical composition as a whole, one can only *conceive* it (or perhaps *imagine* it, in a nonperceptual way). Now one can "perceive the whole" of a piece of music, if one wishes to call it that, by successively perceiving all the parts, as one might also do with a painting of some size, but one cannot do what in the case of a painting is fairly easily done, namely, have a single perceptual experience of it in its entirety. Of course one does not fully *understand* a painting in a single glance, any more than one does a musical piece in a single hearing, but the point is that you can have a synoptic perception, or beholding, of the whole in the former case, but not, given its temporal extent, in the latter.

To grasp a musical work's overall form perceptually would require perceiving in a single mental act the relatedness of numerous temporally distant parts of the work. Since this requirement cannot be met, such relatedness cannot, Gurney reasons, be a primary object of listener attention. The conception or imagination of such relatedness can never be as vivid or gripping as, on the one hand, the perception of the relatedness of parts in a painting at one time, or, on the other hand, the quasi-hearing—a kind of expanded perception—of the relatedness of parts of a musical passage within the compass of aural synthesis. What happens *within* a perception, of a complex sort, is simply of a different order than connections that might exist *between* a perception and something standing *outside* it, such as a memory image of an event long past or well in the future. This contrast, between the experiences possible for and proper to temporally extended artworks, and those possible for and proper to nontemporally extended ones, is a grounding insight of concatenationism.[11]

The importance in music of the present or near-present is, for Gurney, paramount. Even when conscious reflection on a distant past event notice-

---

11. Gurney's intuition here, it is interesting to note, was seconded by a great painter who was his rough contemporary: "Painting is the most beautiful of all the arts . . . like music, it acts on the soul through the intermediary of the senses, harmonious hues corresponding to harmonious sounds, but in painting one obtains a unity that is impossible in music, where the chords come one after the other, and one's judgment is tried by an incessant fatigue if it wishes to unite the beginning and the end" (Paul Gauguin, "Notes synthétiques," quoted in Brettell et al., *Art of Paul Gauguin*, p. 28).

ably colors current audition, Gurney emphasizes, the focus of musical appreciation remains the currently audited part and its immediate musical environment, and not the abstract connection itself, or the earlier term thereof, both of which fail to be encompassable by an act of quasi-hearing centering on the part then being registered. And though perception of a present bit is often overlain by conscious anticipation of a distant future event, the sense of connection to what is remotely to come that is afforded is nowhere as compelling as the grasp one has of a melodic passage in midtrain, whose forward parts are being quasi-heard rather than merely intellectually prehended.

# chapter three

# INITIAL DEFENSE OF
# CONCATENATIONISM

. . . to follow a piece of music as one follows the words of a poem in
a language that one has mastered through and through means the same
. . . as understanding the work itself.
>    —Alban Berg, *Why Is Schoenberg's Music So Difficult to Understand?*

In the primary sense, the listener's real and ultimate response to music
consists not in merely hearing it, but in inwardly reproducing it, and
his understanding of music consists in the ability to do this in his imagination.
>    —Roger Sessions, *The Musical Experience of Composer, Performer, Listener*

Concatenationism, baldly stated as in Chapter 2, seems to call
almost immediately for some qualification. The bulk of this book will in
fact be devoted to considering various worries about concatenationism,
from which those qualifications will proceed. I want to say at the outset,
however, that a concatenationist perspective on musical experience seems
to me to be fundamentally correct. My aim, in subjecting it to scrutiny
and refinement, is ultimately to defend it, not discredit it. But before I
can present it in a version adequate to an educated listener's interaction
with music, and in which an acceptable role is found for intellectual
awareness of musical form, I need first to establish that a concatenationist
position is essentially on the right track. To that end, I review some
intuitions that properly incline us in the direction of concatenationism.
After that we will be in a better position to entertain challenges and correc-
tives.

## Basic Intuitions

One such intuition is what we ordinarily count as *knowing* a piece of music, as *grasping* it, or, in a more vernacular vein, as *getting* it. What seems absolutely crucial to this achievement is tracking the music as it develops at each point, having a sense of where it has just been and where it is now going, perceiving it as a developing process. There is for a listener who knows a piece of music a distinctive experience of involvement in the musical stream. Figuratively, it is as if one were a rafter in the music's midst, responsive to the disturbances of each moment and actively engaged with each turn and twist—as opposed to a distant and passive observer on the banks, insulated from the surrounding flow. The kind of knowing or grasp at issue is fundamentally a matter of attentive absorption in the musical present, of experiencing and responding appropriately to the evolution of the music from point to point, phrase to phrase, and section to section. It is plausible to identify, as the chief ground of this involvement, the capacity to quasi-hear, or aurally synthesize, a small extent of music surrounding any present instant, which synthesizing moves progressively along the length of a piece, binding it part by part, so far as the music allows, into an organic chain.

A comprehending listener is conscious of motion, direction, force, tension, and so on in the succession of tones reaching his ears—that is to say, he hears musical movement in those tones, however that be analyzed, and then, often, gesture and expression in that movement.[1] But his attention is not necessarily drawn to anything remote from the sounding present; he need bring no aural telescope into play, need consult no diagram of the sonic universe in which he is immersed. Instead, what may in general be said of a comprehending listener, one who grasps musical movement and its embodied content, is that he *follows* the music to which he is listening. Following music, or tracking it as it eventuates in time, is I suspect a very large part—perhaps the largest part—of understanding it on the fundamental level. We may note, in the first epigraph to this chapter, the rough concurrence of Alban Berg.[2]

---

1. For elaboration along these lines of what it is to hear a stream of sound as music at all, see Scruton's "Understanding Music."
2. Berg's formulation is presumably meant to cover music of all sorts, Mozart's as well as Schoenberg's.

Following a piece of music, especially one with which one has some familiarity, is often attended by the seconding of the music by the listener, as it were, sotto voce. That is to say, a comprehending listener will often find himself silently singing along with the music he is hearing, a reflection of his involvement in how it very specifically goes. As Roger Sessions suggests in the second epigraph to this chapter, a listener who follows a piece comprehendingly is typically disposed to inwardly parallel the music as he listens.

One measure of a listener's grasp of how a piece goes, which is tied up with his being able to follow it by ear in the most complete manner, is sensitivity to divergences from the proper course of the piece, whether intentionally or accidentally brought about, and whether in melodic, harmonic, timbral, dynamic, or other respects.[3] Such alteration-detection sensitivity in regard to a given piece of music can be accounted a strong, if defeasible, sign of basic musical understanding of the piece. It signals, for one, that the listener has grasped the piece as the distinct musical individual that it is.[4]

The centrality of following or tracking, in the sense I have been highlighting, is something that distinguishes music from narrative arts, such as novel or film, where some degree of reflection on and review of extended portions of material is requisite for even the most basic understanding of what has been presented. By contrast, basic understanding in music, whose essence is the involved following or tracking of musical process, need entail no awareness of form writ large, for example, tonal plan, thematic scheme, or sectional structure. No notion of a piece's global pattern or even a single large-scale relation connecting distant portions of a piece need cross the listener's mind. When irrespective of any architectonic awareness that may be present a piece of music coheres for a listener from moment to moment and is

---

3. Of course there is a level of insignificance below which such divergences will not be remarked, or will be accepted as within the bounds of normal performative interpretation of the piece.

4. I here leave aside historical and contextual considerations that must be acknowledged in working out a proper ontology of musical works, which somewhat complicate the idea of the individual that is a piece of music. See my "What a Musical Work Is" and "What a Musical Work Is, Again."

followed absorbedly and responsively as it unfolds, we can say that the listener has come to know the piece, to basically understand it, by ear. If a listener can track a piece aurally from beginning to end it can, it seems, be said to "make sense" to him, whatever his evaluation of that "sense" turns out to be.

If imaginative contemplation need play no part at this basic level, if intellectual apprehension of stretches of music need not occur, if cognizance of overarching form seems optional, then what of necessity *does* occupy consciousness in any instance of comprehending listening? Gurney's answer strikes me as roughly on the mark: the listener is focused on individual parts as they occur, and on the connections of such parts with immediately preceding and succeeding parts. If appropriate expectations and response capacities are in place, focus of this local sort seems to suffice for comprehending listening. Attention may very well not carry, in such listening, beyond what constitutes the moment, thickly construed—that is, the currently unfolding musical event with its expanding and contracting penumbra.

Further confirmation that Gurney locates the essence of musical understanding in the right place, that is, in the grasp of more or less moment-to-moment connections, is provided by the phenomenon of a piece *not* "making sense" to a listener. When someone claims that some composition, say, a string quartet by Schoenberg, does not "make sense" to him, this is invariably a matter of being unable to follow the musical logic from point to point. It is a matter of being unable to hear in such a way as to be inside the music, registering and responding to implications and realizations, instead of outside it, noting its passing but experiencing no aural involvement in where it has been or where it is going. A piece typically "makes no sense" to a listener when he is unable to find it coherent on a small scale, when he is unable to perceive local connections, when he cannot make successive events fit together in his ear, when he cannot become absorbed in the music's developing present. A listener might, on the other hand, find the large-scale organization of such a piece intelligible, even readily apparent on listening, but that will be of no consequence if the music never congeals for him on a moment-to-moment basis. If something like quasi-hearing never takes place, the music remains largely "senseless" for a listener, regardless of what large-scale formal insights may occur.[5]

.    .    .

A second intuition favoring concatenationism is this. One of the clearest indications that one has understood a piece of music at a basic level is one's ability to *reproduce* parts of it in some manner—by playing, singing, humming, or whistling it—or relatedly, one's knowing how a given bit is to be continued, or what bit succeeds the bit that has just occurred. Such abilities, to reproduce or continue the musical substance of a piece, are clear testimony to a person's comprehending absorption in musical progression while listening on prior occasions. They are not, however, any indication that a person has engaged in conscious cognition of overall form or of large-scale formal relationships. If reproductive or continuational ability is admitted to be strong evidence of basic musical understanding, of someone's having basically grasped a piece of music, then it seems reasonable that such understanding consists, at core, in tacitly knowing just how a piece goes from point to point. One listens with understanding when one actively registers and projects musical movement at each instant, with this understanding being reflected, as a rule, in the capacity to later give back, in some fashion, that musical movement. However, as it seems that such understanding is not inevitably so reflected, in all individuals, it would be wrong to account reproductive or continuational ability a strictly necessary condition for basic musical understanding. Even so, it may be about the surest indicator of it that we have.

Of course, *mere* reproduction will not serve as a mark of even the sort of basic understanding we are concerned with, but only reproduction of a *musical* sort—to use the musician's perhaps favorite term of praise. Reproduction that is purely mechanical, bespeaking perhaps only eidetic

---

5. Schoenberg, incidentally, seems to have conceived of composition in a way that suggests he might well have agreed that musical comprehension was fundamentally concatenationist in nature: "Schoenberg argues that one of the basic problems composers must address is how to join different musical events together in such a way that the result can be coherent. For Schoenberg, coherence must be grounded in some kind of repetition. When different pitches, rhythms and other components are joined together into some kind of characteristic pattern, they form the fundamental building blocks of musical thought" (Ethan Haimo, review of *The Musical Idea and the Logic, Technique, and Art of Its Presentation,* by Arnold Schoenberg, *Times Literary Supplement,* May 31, 1996).

memory for sounds, or reproduction that fails to reflect a grasp of the feeling, tension, or flow proper to the music being reproduced, is admittedly no sign of understanding. But generally one can tell from a person's reproductive efforts if he has heard the music roughly as it should be heard, rather than as either a brute succession of notes, or as containing gestures or expression foreign to it. (The latter might characterize the first-time hearing of Beethoven or Brahms by a musically talented listener from a nonwestern culture. The former might characterize the hearing of a hypothetical robotic listener possessed of a low-grade digital processor.)

Even virtuoso players—for instance, Vladimir Horowitz—may sometimes reproduce (i.e., perform) music in such a way as to make us doubt whether their prior hearings of the music amounted to even basic understanding. On balance, though, we would probably allow that they did, and simply write such performances off to either bad taste or bad judgment or both—which are sins narrowly compatible with basic aural comprehension of music.

So I think we can rest in the observation that reproductive or continuational ability of at least minimal musicality, in regard to music heard, is a compelling sign of basic musical understanding of it. But such abilities seem quite readily acquired through nothing more than repeated, present-focused listening of a concatenationist sort.

. . .

A third intuition supportive of concatenationism concerns the matter of the emotional content or quality of a piece of music. I suggest that present-focused hearing, of the sort I have been profiling, is in the main sufficient for perceiving such content and for responding to it appropriately. To a properly prepared auditor—that is, one with an adequate listening background and stylistic attunement—the emotional effect of a piece will be substantially conveyed by the individual bits and the transitions between them, and the emotional qualities the piece is assessed to have will largely be ones that can be said to attach to or reside in those bits and transitions. The emotional content of music, in other words, is not primarily communicated to a listener by large-scale formal relations, consciously apprehended, but instead by suitably arranged parts small enough to fall within the scope of quasi-hearing.

The strutting confidence of the opening of Schubert's Piano Trio in B-flat, the explosive vitality of the opening of Beethoven's Eighth

Symphony, the warm lightheartedness of the opening of Mozart's Piano
Concerto No. 23 in A, the deep despondency of the opening of Schoenberg's *Verklärte Nacht*—examples might be multiplied indefinitely—
can be heard in them in moments, in the space of a few bars. (I speak,
of course, of the expressiveness itself, not of its labeling.) The stretches
of music in which expressive content resides are, for the most part,
ones well within the range of what can be grasped aurally; intellectual
apprehension of relationships across larger temporal spans need not
enter in.

Insofar as this observation is correct, it provides further reason to think
that what is fundamental in understanding music can be accounted for
by concatenationist lights. Certainly if you do not grasp the flow, motion,
and directedness of music on a primary level—if you have no quasi-
hearing experience of it—you cannot hear its expressiveness, that is,
construe its movement in terms of some feeling, attitude, or emotion.
But it is not clear that anything *more* is required, for example, of a
synoptic or reflective sort, in order for a listener to register and respond
to at least the great bulk of emotional content in music.[6]

. . .

Thus, at least three broad intuitions—the close connection of following and understanding in music, the probative value of musical reproductive or continuational ability, and the localized nature of most musical
expressiveness—lend support to a concatenationist picture of basic musical understanding. Adopting that picture, then, I here wager the
claim—to be revisited and reassessed throughout this book—that insight
into large-scale form simply does not enter into the basic understanding
of music, that such understanding can thus be attained without any
awareness whatsoever of overall structure. Furthermore, if one has
grasped a piece of music aurally, subsequently apprehending its overall
form will not lead one to think that one had not really grasped the music
before. Formal awareness of large-scale relations may be required for
understanding how a piece is constructed, and perhaps why it is effective
as music, but that is different from understanding the piece itself—that

6. For analysis of the concept of emotional content in music, see my "Musical Expressiveness."

is, achieving basic musical understanding of it.[7] If this is so, then it seems Gurney is right that the architectonic aspect of a piece of music, far from being a preeminent object of musical attention, might rather be ignored by a listener with impunity.

### Musical Understanding

Understanding music, as a number of philosophers have recently observed, is fundamentally a matter of hearing it a certain way.[8] Most abstractly put, I claim, that way of hearing is one that involves aurally connecting together tones currently sounding, ones just sounded, and ones about to come, synthesizing them into a flow as far as possible at every point. And this, in essence, means quasi-hearing some stretch of variable length surrounding the notes one is currently hearing.

If basic musical understanding can be identified with a locally synthetic rather than globally synoptic manner of hearing, then it is conceivable that with musical compositions, even complicated and lengthy ones, we miss nothing crucial by staying, as it were, in the moment, following the development of events in real time, engaging in no conscious mental activity of wider scope that has the whole or some extended portion of it as object. Of course it is rare that activity of that sort is entirely absent, but the point is that its contribution to basic understanding may be nil.

It is common in discussions of musical understanding to distinguish between understanding in the sense of *knowing that* and understanding in the sense of *knowing how*.[9] The first consists in propositional knowledge—for example, knowing that the key of the *Eroica* Symphony is E-flat major—while the second arguably does not, but consists rather in

---

7. In the same vein we might observe that why a piece offers a cogent listening experience, why it allows for the scope of quasi-hearing it does, or why it is so moving, are not the objects of basic musical understanding, but rather, of the understanding of basic musical understanding.

8. See, for instance, Scruton, "Analytical Philosophy and the Meaning of Music"; Budd, "Understanding Music"; Kraut, "Perceiving the Music Correctly"; and Ridley, *Music, Value, and the Passions,* chap. 3.

9. See, for example, the discussion in Stephen Davies, *Musical Meaning and Expression,* pp. 337–340.

demonstrable abilities, in being able to do this or that in regard to some music or other.

In this respect, the notion of basic musical understanding pursued here, whose core is the responsive following of music and whose basis is the phenomenon of quasi-hearing, is more nearly a matter of knowing how than of knowing that. To have basic understanding of a piece of music is to have the ability to hear it in a certain way; thus, somewhat liberally, it is to know *how* to hear the music, *how* to experience it in listening.[10] Such know-how, if we may call it that, is built up from prior hearings of the piece in question, while resting on a background of hearing competence derived from the hearing of music in the given tradition generally. Alternatively, basic musical understanding of a piece could be said to be essentially a matter of knowing how the music goes, where that knowledge is exhibited in various perceptual, recognitional, and continuational capacities in regard to a piece, rather than as a command of true propositions about the piece's course. But knowing how the music goes, in that sense, is tantamount to knowing how to hear it—that is, being able to hear it—in a certain way.

Now there is also, at first blush, what may be called acquaintance knowledge of a piece of music, as when one is said to know an individual person or place. Acquaintance knowledge might seem to be what is inquired about when one asks, for example, "Do you know Brahms's Violin Concerto?" A reasonable gloss of that question would be "Are you familiar with [that is, acquainted with] Brahms's Violin Concerto?"

But it is very likely that such musical acquaintance knowledge is reducible to forms of musical knowing how or being able. For consider how we would naturally construe positive answers to the preceding question. "Yes, I do" might be constructed, roughly, as "I can, in virtue of past hearing, recognize it readily enough," while "Yes, very well" might be construed, roughly, as "I can recognize and reproduce, after a fashion, many parts of it." If there is an aspect of acquaintance knowledge that is not so reducible, it would seem to be the mere fact of having heard,

---

10. Admittedly, *knowing how to x* usually implies, at least conversationally, that *x* is something one does actively and deliberately, while *being able to x* lacks such implication. But I will overlook any such shades of meaning in the present discussion.

or having been exposed to, a given piece of music. But where such hearing leaves no trace, in terms of *any* sort of capacity vis-à-vis future hearings of a piece, there would seem little warrant for calling the mere fast of exposure to the piece musical knowledge of any sort.[11]

There is a further ambiguity in the idea of someone's understanding of a piece of music that should be acknowledged at this point. A person's understanding of a piece of music is, in the first instance, an acquired and standing *ability* vis-à-vis that piece of music, an ability to hear it a certain way, and so is something that one possesses, for example, even while asleep. Call this *dispositional* understanding. But a person's understanding of a piece may also, in the second instance, be construed as the actual *exercise* of that ability as the piece is being audited. Call that *occurrent* understanding. Thus, on the first construal I can be said, on the basis of past experience, to understand the *Eroica* even though I am not now listening to it. On the second construal I can be said to be understanding the *Eroica* as, and only as, I am now hearing it in a particular way. There will usually be no problem in practice about which sense of musical understanding is in view, the dispositional or the oc-current.

Of course, much of what constitutes the dispositional understanding of a piece in a familiar idiom will be present in the listener prior even to hearing the piece for the first time. That is to say, much of the capacity to hear in the right way will already be present in virtue of the listener's general attunement to the style in question. However, the capacity with which we can identify reasonably full aural comprehension of a piece of music—involving substantial quasi-hearing, detailed grasp of musical fabric, vivid anticipation of musical evolution, and developed emotional responsiveness—clearly requires *some* prior exposure to the actual course of a piece in listening, no matter how familiar its idiom. The music must, so to speak, get into one's ears, however effortlessly that occurs in some cases. This is why I spoke earlier of a listener's standing musical under-standing, in the piece-specific sense, as an *acquired* capacity, notwith-

11. Compare: if you had once encountered someone, but without any subsequent recollection of the meeting or any changed disposition toward the person as a result, it would be exceedingly odd to say that you knew him, or were acquainted with him, merely because you had once been in perceptual contact with him.

standing the fact that the general capacities that serve as background to such specific understandings will already be in place.

· · ·

The notion of basic musical understanding limned here is one I will invoke regularly in what follows. It will not have escaped notice that I have not defined that notion explicitly, but have instead contented myself with sketching its identifying marks. My hope, though, is that the sketch is one whose subject most music lovers will recognize.[12]

The marks of basic musical understanding noted so far were these: present-centered absorption in musical flow; active following of musical progression; inward seconding of musical movement; sensitivity to musical alteration; reproductive ability; continuational ability; and grasp of emotional expression. Others might be added, and one in fact suggests itself immediately: pleasure in listening, at least when that pleasure is taken in the right thing, namely the quality of the musical substance heard in all its particularity. Further, it seems clear that such pleasure in musical process does not require, in the vast majority of cases, anything beyond attention to that process in its moment-by-moment evolution. So that would give us, at a minimum, eight marks of basic musical understanding, none of which appears to implicate mental activity of a more than concatenationist sort.[13]

12. It might be thought that the great diversity of music, even within the Western tradition, and thus the diversity of conditions that might reasonably be held to be necessary for the understanding of particular pieces, would militate against any unitary picture of basic musical understanding. But as Malcolm Budd has rightly observed, if one's aim is suitably restricted, there is no harm in offering a single model of the phenomenon: "the fact that musical understanding does not have an essence does not imply that it does not have a common core—the understanding of music's intrinsic, non-referential nature" ("Understanding Music," p. 237).
13. This count should not be taken too seriously, as it could obviously be raised or lowered, depending on how finely one individuated the abilities or experiential traits in question. I have been pleased to discover that Frank Sibley, the great British aesthetician, proposed some marks of basic musical understanding very similar to those focused on here: "To have grasped the character of a piece of music might involve any of many abilities: to recognize it again, to recall in your head roughly how it went, to know if it is wrongly played next time (but not necessarily those; you might have poor musical memory); to whistle parts of it (but not if you cannot whistle); to know, when whistling it, when you have got it wrong, without necessarily being able to correct it; to realize what harmonies are lost in whistling; to know, when it is being played, that an oboe or a new motif will shortly enter": "Making Music Our Own," pp. 173–74.

Perhaps we could, though, make a division among these marks, between those actually constitutive of, or elements in the experience of, basic musical understanding and those that, though strong indicators of its presence, are not strictly part and parcel of it. Thus we might reasonably assign present-centered absorption and active following—both underwritten by the phenomenon of quasi-hearing—and grasp of expressiveness to the first category, while assigning to the second category alteration sensitivity, reproductive ability, continuational ability, seconding propensity, and listening enjoyment. The marks in this second group are strong indicators of the occurrence of basic musical understanding because they are, at least with music of some worth, the usual consequences or concomitants of such understanding. Certainly the absence of any of them is prima facie, if not conclusive, evidence that basic musical understanding has not occurred.

When I speak subsequently of basic musical understanding, I will sometimes have in mind the elements we might regard as strictly constitutive of it as a particular way of hearing, or being engaged by, music—that is, active following, present-centered absorption, and registering of emotional content—while at other times I will have in mind the broader picture sketched, in which those constitutive elements are joined by the other marks noted that are almost invariably present as well.

The adjective "basic" in the phrase "basic musical understanding" carries some suggestions that I endorse and others that I would prefer to exorcise. I mean to convey that such understanding is essential (to any apprehension of music), fundamental (to any further musical understanding), and central (to worthwhile musical experience of any kind)—but not that it is simple, or elementary, or rudimentary. While characterizing basic musical understanding as constituting ideal understanding of music would be going too far, such understanding does represent, I claim, a level of understanding substantially adequate to most instrumental music in the Western tradition.

Roger Scruton has proposed, following Wittgenstein, that the meaning of music in essence be construed as whatever it is we understand when we understand it.[14] If so, then anything that deserves to be called basic

---

14. See Scruton, "Analytical Philosophy and the Meaning of Music" and "Notes on the Meaning of Music."

*understanding* of music should accordingly be adequate to all it would be natural to account part of music's basic *meaning*. Intuitively, it seems there are basically two main aspects of meaning, of what it is that we understand, in music. One concerns the purely internal connectedness of music, its kinetic and dynamic content: this is music perceived or interpreted as tonal process. The other concerns the expressive side of music, the gestural, emotive, and dramatic content embodied in tonal process: this is music perceived or interpreted in terms of body, life, and world. Now if what I have pointed to as basic musical understanding is largely adequate to permit grasp of both musical movement and extramusical expression, then it would be fair to conclude that it is, as desired, correlative with basic musical meaning. I submit that this is indeed the case.

. . .

I record here a number of additional caveats apropos of this notion of basic musical understanding, some of which have already been touched on. One caveat is that it is the sort of core understanding that is appropriate to, and called forth by, the mainstream of Western instrumental music, from Bach to Schoenberg.[15] This is music guided for the most part by ideals or norms of continuation, progression, development, evolution, and directionality. Leonard Meyer has labeled such music teleological, in contrast to the antiteleological, non-goal-oriented variety essayed by composers such as John Cage and Karlheinz Stockhausen.[16] Music that does not present the aspect of a directed process of some sort—music that presents itself instead as a series of unrelated sonic events, a found object, or as militantly nondevelopmental—is not music for which what I have described would count as core understanding. Such music would seem to call for a kind of comprehension or response that is almost the opposite of the sort of involvement teleological music requires and standardly elicits. The extent to which what I have identified as the core

15. Or perhaps more inclusively, Byrd to Shostakovitch. Incidentally, I do not mean to exclude—though I will generally not discuss—music organized atonally or dodecaphonically. But there is every reason to think that if concatenationism is adequate to the basic comprehension of tonal music, properly speaking, it would prove adequate to the basic comprehension of atonal and dodecaphonic music as well.
16. Or, to a much lesser extent, Steve Reich and Philip Glass. See Meyer, *Music, the Arts, and Ideas,* chap. 5.

understanding experience in the case of classical music plays the same sort of role in the understanding of other sorts of music is an open question. I would think, though, that something like that experience would be present with any teleological, progressive music in which events are produced and are to be heard in vivid relation to those that immediately precede them. Surely this music would include, for example, rock, jazz, flamenco, Indian music, African drumming, and so on.[17]

A second caveat is this: basic musical understanding naturally does not preclude, but is rather compatible with, any other kind of legitimate understanding that may also supervene on an occasion of comprehending listening. Among sorts of understanding not comprised in basic musical understanding, for example, are grasping the representational content of program music, registering the social or political significance some music may manage to possess, or recognizing principles governing a piece of music as revealed by some analytic procedure. It is likely, however, both that additional kinds of understanding such as these are generally impossible without basic musical understanding and that even if they were attainable without such understanding, they would in any event have little point; that is to say, they would be unrewarding, abstract determinations with no experiential impact.[18]

A third caveat: the sort of experience that is at the heart of basic musical understanding—the synthesizing of sounds present to the ears over a short span, or the quasi-hearing of short stretches of music—only truly constitutes an understanding of that music if it occurs in a listener appropriately informed and backgrounded as to the nature of the piece he is auditing, for example, its period, genre, and instrumentation. When a listener who attends with the right sort of mental set has the kind of

17. Pierre Boulez, speaking of Debussy's *Jeux*, has this to say: "far from being miserably disjointed, the structure, which is rich in invention and of a fluctuating complexity, initiates an extremely tensile form of thought, based on the notion of irreversible movement; to hear it, one has only to submit to its development, for the constant evolution of the thematic ideas thrusts aside all symmetry in the architecture. . . . *Jeux* marks the advent of a musical form which, instantly renewing itself, involves a no less instantaneous mode of listening" (liner notes, *Boulez Conducts Debussy*, Columbia D3M-32988, 1974). What Boulez is saying about *Jeux* and the sort of attention it calls for from a listener might be said, if concatenationism is valid, for all music of a teleological sort, even if *Jeux* is unusual in so thoroughly shortcircuiting the attempt either to analyze or to audit it architectonically.
18. For a valuable discussion of different levels of understanding music and their interdependencies, see Michael Tanner, "Understanding Music."

quasi-hearing experience apt for a given piece, then basic musical under-standing may be said to occur, but not necessarily otherwise. In other words, the characteristic experience must involve the right sorts of expec-tations and tendencies to respond, rooted in an implicit grasp of the type of the piece in question, or else it is only a simulacrum of understanding, as the cogencies and connections that appear within the experience may not be those proper to the piece when correctly apprehended.[19]

.   .   .

Before proceeding, I address some remarks of John Sloboda, a leading psychologist of music, which seem at face value to directly contra-dict what concatenationism insists on:

> In defence of such research [on the hearing of brief segments of music] one may, of course, argue that music is made up of a large number of small fragments chained together, and that music perception is simply a concatenation of a series of perceptual acts on such fragments. If so, however, then all the art of classical composition must go for nothing, because, as has been argued earlier, events quite far apart in time can be intimately connected structurally. Intelligent listening, we may argue, picks up such relationships; it spans large numbers of notes so as to be "structural hearing." . . . Composers write for listeners, not analysts, and the testimony of many listeners is that they *can* discern the large-scale relationships that analysts characterize.[20]

There are, in my view, two questionable points in the above. One is the fallacious inference to the futility of compositional thought from the supposition that music is essentially experienced concatenationally. This inference arises from not distinguishing between the issue of the *causal* relevance of musical relationships, and that of their *appreciative* relevance for a listener—something I will take up in the following chapter. That far-flung events can be structurally related, and that this relation may affect a listener's musical processing, does not entail that a listener com-

19. For useful admonitions on this point, see Scruton, "Understanding Music"; Budd, "Understanding Music"; and my "Musical Literacy."
20. John Sloboda, *The Musical Mind*, p. 152.

prehending the events in such relation must leave the level of part-by-part apprehension and carry conscious attention to that relation.

The second questionable point is an ambiguity in how the phrase "picks up such relationships," used to characterize intelligent listening, can be understood. If registering on some level, implying an interaction between memory representations and present perceptions, is all that is meant, then there is no necessary conflict with concatenationist principles. But if "picks up such relationships" is meant to denote an intellectual activity, involving explicit reflection on or synoptic contemplation of some musical expanse, then there is indeed some conflict. Sloboda notes, fairly enough, that many listeners *can* discern large-scale relationships in music; but that hardly shows either that they regularly *do* do so when absorbed in music comprehendingly, or that there is any *need* to do so in order to achieve basic musical comprehension.

Nicholas Cook, however, seems to endorse Sloboda's basic message, which he takes to be illustrated by the perception of harp glissandos and violin runs: "It seems clear that here, at least, the perception of the musical event as a whole—the swoosh of the harp, the violin scale—is a primary perceptual construct, rather than the concatenation of a series of fragmentary perceptual acts.[21]

But clearly, we have no quarrel with that observation; musical perception is indeed not a summation of individual acts of registering single tones. The issue is joined rather at the level of significantly larger units, such as periods, sections, and movements. These units, whatever underlying structural relations hold them together, cannot be grasped in single perceptions of broad scope, and so must be encompassed, in effect, through a concatenation—though one with continually forming and dissolving links—of musical stretches that *are* grasped perceptually as wholes. Concatenationism is not the view that musical apprehension involves integrating individually perceived notes or intervals into phrases, though of course that occurs, but the view that what musical apprehension centrally involves is integrating individually perceived phrases, melodies, or sequences into a progressively traversed musical totality.

---

21. Cook, *Music, Imagination, and Culture,* p. 155. Cook is an author I will call on often as a witness friendly to concatenationism, though his own arguments are not directed specifically to that conclusion.

### Gurney and Other Theorists

Gurney's views can be usefully compared, at this juncture, with those of the contemporary music theorist Leonard Meyer. It would not be unreasonable to see Meyer's work as broadly in the Gurneyan tradition. Both theorists advocate above all a dynamic, developmental approach to musical form, as opposed to an atemporal and architectonic one of the sort favored in a crude vein by sectional analysts, and in a more sophisticated vein by Schenkerian ones.

For both Gurney and Meyer, the most important aspect of musical experience is the sense of continuation and progression felt at each point, the apprehension in present events of directions and tendencies with respect to imminent events, and the various kinds of rightness of each event with respect to its immediately preceding context. Where Gurney speaks of cogency of sequence of bit upon bit, Meyer speaks of the realization or nonrealization by later events of implications inherent in earlier ones.[22] Both theorists emphasize the succession of part on part, the relation of consequent to antecedent, as constituting the fabric of music; neither accords much importance to broad synoptic vistas in which every element is in its place for apprehension all at once.

Meyer views a musical work as a series of events, apprehended sequentially by a listener, in which the apprehension of earlier events has a marked effect on the apprehension of later events. This effect comes about primarily through formation of new expectations, and modification of existing expectations, that the listener has for the future course of the music. Later events then satisfy or frustrate, in varying degrees, the expectations generated by the perception of earlier events. The experience of these later events is then affectively colored in virtue of what has been apprehended before. And every arriving event becomes a generator of

---

22. In earlier writings, such as *Emotion and Meaning in Music,* Meyer was inclined to speak of the fulfillment or frustration of listeners' expectations by the course of musical events. A preference for "objective" over "subjective" terminology induced him to abandon expectation talk in later writings, such as *Music, the Arts, and Ideas* and *Explaining Music.* But it seems clear that talk of the implications that one musical event has for another will ultimately have to be cashed out "subjectively," in terms of expectations generated in a properly attuned listener, or alternatively in terms of the assessments of probability which a properly attuned listener subconsciously makes about what events will follow those he is hearing at any point. This last, further, might be given a behavioristic gloss in terms of surprise or discomfort reactions attendant on various continuations.

expectations, which may or may not be fulfilled, for events still later in the course of the piece.

But there are, not surprisingly, several differences between Meyer's perspective and Gurney's. It will be helpful to take note of them here, as the issues raised by these differences will come up, in one form or another, in the general discussion of concatenationism that lies ahead.

First, Meyer stresses the influence that *all* the earlier events in a piece have on a listener's sense of what will follow the event he is currently auditing or, alternately, on what the implications of the present event are. Now, Gurney does not deny that what one has heard earlier in a piece affects one's assessment of cogency of sequence of one bit on another in current experience. But neither does he recognize its relevance very clearly. A second difference is this: cogency of sequence, the primary ground of musical worth for Gurney, is a matter of rightness of continuation, of the joining of one part to another in organic union, characterized by something like subjective "necessity." Now, this condition would appear to correspond just to Meyer's *most probable* consequent at each point in a piece, for what else will seem so right, so cogent, so "necessary"? It is not clear that Gurney's emphasis on the inevitability of good continuations leaves room for one of Meyer's central observations—that music is often interesting and good precisely because it does *not* take the most likely course. Sometimes, in fact, it is the least "inevitable" continuation that is ultimately the most rewarding.

Third, although Meyer might agree with Gurney that the primary focus of listening consciousness is the shifting boundary between the bit just heard and the one to come, Meyer is concerned not only with implications that present bits or passages have for the bits or passages that immediately succeed them, but also with implications between present bits and ones at some distance removed, and implications between larger units, such as paragraphs, sections, and even whole movements. In other words, on Meyer's view one's sense of the dynamic progression of a piece of music—of its tendencies and directions—is not confined, as it is for Gurney, to what are essentially small-scale, moment-to-moment connections. Meyer tries to allow for hierarchic ordering of implicative forces on different levels.[23] Furthermore, according to Meyer there are often *aware-*

---

23. Especially in *Explaining Music*.

*nesses* of distant connections, such as closures or resolutions of earlier patterns, which form part of the complete understanding of a piece of music.

Finally, Meyer does acknowledge, as musically relevant, contemplation of a piece as a whole—of a network of implications and realizations—after listening is completed. Meyer's *evident* meanings involve reflection on earlier events in light of what is currently being heard, and his *determinate* meanings are accessible to reflection only after the piece has presented itself in its entirety and its various hypothetical (prospective) meanings and evident (retrospective) meanings can be grasped in relation to one another.[24] So though there is a degree of convergence between Meyer's perspective on music and Gurney's, those perspectives are by no means coincident. Still, the similarity in spirit between Gurney and Meyer is unmistakable.

Meyer is not the only more recent musical thinker of note to endorse aspects of what Gurney emphatically urged about musical experience. Edward Cone is another theorist whose writings evidence sympathy, albeit partial, for Gurney's ideas. Consider these remarks, from a 1968 essay on aesthetic appreciation:

> The mode by which we directly perceive the sensuous medium, its primitive elements, and their closest interrelationships, is one I wish to contrast with that of synoptic comprehension. I shall call it the mode of *immediate apprehension.* . . . Synoptic comprehension is to some extent conceptual: it is our realization of the form of what we have perceived. . . . Of the two modes, it is the immediate that enjoys both temporal and logical priority in our perception of art . . . logical, because, in my view, enjoyment of such apprehension can lead to some measure of esthetic satisfaction whether or not it is accompanied by synoptic comprehension, and whether or not such comprehension, if achieved, finds a worthy object.[25]

Of course, Cone's qualified approval here of a recognizably Gurneyan point of view is no mere accident. His sympathetic introduction to the

24. See Meyer, *Emotion and Meaning in Music,* pp. 35–38.
25. Cone, "On Two Modes of Esthetic Perception," in *Musical Form and Musical Performance,* pp. 89–90.

1966 reprint of Gurney's *Power of Sound* would lead one to expect as much. Cone's sympathy with the Gurneyan line on listening is in fact explicitly reaffirmed in the 1968 essay from which I have just quoted, in the following additional remark: "I readily admit to such a lust [for musical structure], but I must also confess an equally unholy delight in what Edmund Gurney calls 'the successive notes and fragments, as they turn up moment after moment, throughout any piece of music which is keenly and characteristically enjoyed.'"[26]

Another important musical thinker, of somewhat earlier vintage, in whom one can discern more than a trace of Gurneyan disposition—though whether this reflects actual acquaintance with *The Power of Sound* I cannot say—is Donald Francis Tovey. As is well known, one of Tovey's central tenets was that everything of aesthetic importance in music lay within the province of what he called "the naive listener," one with sensibility, experience, and willing ears, but no particular musical training.[27] Tovey held that if something in the large-scale formal organization of a composition was of aesthetic importance, the composer worth his salt would see to it that it could be grasped in the small, unreflectingly, by this "naive" listener: "while the listener must not expect to hear the whole contents of a piece of music at once, nothing concerns him that will not ultimately reach his ear either as a directly audible fact or as a cumulative satisfaction in things of which the hidden foundations are well and truly laid."[28]

For Tovey, as for Gurney, a piece of music remains something deeply temporal, to which our access is unavoidably sequential, and any adequate representation of musical experience must do justice to that fact:

The first condition for a correct analysis of any piece of music is that the composition must be regarded as a process in time. There is no

26. Ibid., p. 97. In a later essay, "Three Ways of Reading a Detective Story—or a Brahms Intermezzo," Cone castigates what he calls "Second-Hearing"—that is, atemporal—analysis of music, which, as he says, "does scant justice to our experience of hearing a composition in real time" (p. 86). He also puts his finger nicely on the inherent conflict between musical absorption and synoptic reflection: "when we listen intently to music, the immediacy of what we are hearing makes it difficult or impossible for us to entertain other *musical* ideas at the same time" (p. 85).
27. For a useful discussion of Tovey's musical aesthetics, see Joseph Kerman, "Tovey's Beethoven."
28. Tovey, *Essays in Musical Analysis*, 1:18–19.

such thing as a simultaneous musical *coup d'oeil;* not even though Mozart is believed to have said that he imagined his music in that way.[29] Any musical terminology must be wrong if it assumes a map-like or space-like view of music instead of a time-like view.[30]

This cursory review of some of Gurney's successors suffices to show, at least, that Gurney has not been entirely alone in his instincts concerning what is crucial in the comprehension of music. So it would be wrong to paint him as wholly a voice in the wilderness. But the dominance of architectonicist and intellectualist approaches to musical comprehension prompts one to turn up the volume on that voice. If Tovey, Cone, and Meyer are any indication, that voice may yet find more echo among the musically concerned than it has so far found.

29. Tovey, *Companion to Beethoven's Pianoforte Sonatas,* Introduction.
30. Tovey, *Essays in Musical Analysis,* I:11.

# chapter four

# CONCATENATIONISM AND CAUSALITY

Our love of music is bound up with its forward motion; nonetheless it
is precisely the creation of that sense of flow, its interrelation with and
resultant effect upon formal structure, that calls forth high intellectual
capacities of a composer and offers keen pleasures for listening minds.
    —Aaron Copland, *The Pleasures of Music*

$M$y objective in this chapter is to bring out some of the common
ground shared by concatenationism, the view I have derived from Gurney,
and the architectonicism to which it is opposed. Everyone, Gurney included, must allow that the large-scale organization of a piece affects a
listener's experience in *some* manner. Though it never becomes an object
of perception itself, its being the way it is must have some effect on a
listener's resulting experience. In particular, the earlier portions of a piece,
through being heard, must invariably influence apprehension of later
parts not contiguous with them. Musical comprehension cannot be a
purely atomistic affair looked at from this angle.

### What Concatenationism Cannot Deny

Now it is the appreciative, and not the causal, role of large-scale
form that is my main concern in this essay. Still, the question of the
extent to which large-scale as opposed to small-scale relationships are
causally potent in shaping the quality of music as heard from point to point
is an important one, and of independent interest. Concatenationism, as
I have construed it, though basically a view about the nature of compre-

hending listening and the kinds of awarenesses involved therein, is perhaps intuitively allied with, though not logically bound to, the thesis that large-scale connections make less of a causal contribution to the experience of music than do small-scale connections.[1] As a matter of fact, I am inclined to think that that is true. Nevertheless, that a piece's large-scale organization makes some causal contribution to, or has some bearing on, the listener's resulting experience seems virtually undeniable.

.    .    .

On first glance, one might take concatenationism to be maintaining the following: "What has occurred, or will occur, in parts of a piece of music not currently being aurally grasped is simply of no importance whatsoever—only the present and its immediate connections fore and aft matter at all." But that would be a caricature of the view, and an unwarranted one. A concatenationist does not wish to deny the effect that having heard earlier parts of a piece has on the way a present bit is experienced. Nor does he wish to deny that the patterning of events already past influences the reception accorded a bit currently being heard. Of course the rest of a composition and how it is structured may be causally relevant, through medium- and long-term memory, to the experience of any given part. Concatenationists do not gainsay this proposition, though they may tend to downplay its importance. What they primarily question is whether listening to music with comprehension calls for *active awareness* of anything outside the quasi-present—regions of a piece far from that in which the listener is currently engaged, for example, or links to events remote from that which is currently being heard. Concatenationists also question whether such awareness affords any significant satisfaction in its own right, and whether it is crucial to evaluating the worth of a musical work. In short, for concatentationists, it is the role of *thought* or *reflection* on distant events and large-scale structure that is mainly in contention, not the role of those parts and that structure *tout court*. The

1. Gurney certainly could not have believed that the only things causally relevant to grasping a current bit are the immediately preceding or succeeding measures. But he does at least seem to want to affirm a lesser causal importance for the outlying surround of a bit in comparison to its immediate neighborhood. One formulation of the claim that seems implicit in Gurney's text would be this: temporally remote connections to a given bit are generally less influential, as regards perceived character (e.g. impressiveness, cogency), than temporally near connections to the given bit.

effect of the whole of a piece and its overall organization on the experience of any part cannot seriously be questioned. But whether conscious grasp of the whole or its underlying organization is required for understanding a piece's content and assessing its value is, from a concatenationist's perspective, very much in question.

In order to focus more clearly what cannot reasonably be disputed about the process of basic musical comprehension, it will be helpful to review, with a concrete example, some ways in which the parts of a composition not then being perceived plausibly affect the perception of a part then present. Consider the Polonaise from J. S. Bach's Orchestral Suite No. 2 in b minor for Flute and Strings (figure 1), a simple yet elegantly crafted dance movement, and assume that this is the third or so auditioning of the piece by a knowledgeable listener.[2] Though this is a relatively short piece of music, about four minutes in length, it is long enough to illustrate the causal bearing of structural relationships on the listener's experience.

Before the first note is heard, then, we have a listener who has certain expectations, though not necessarily conscious ones, as to what he will hear. These expectations derive principally from two sources. One source is past experience of other pieces related to Bach's suite, in particular ones from the same period or in a similar style. Such experience clearly leaves an imprint on the listener that is capable of shaping the pattern of his responses to music subsequently heard. The knowledge that one is to hear a certain genre of piece typically activates this imprint, generating expectancies of various sorts.[3] A second, more obvious source of a listener's expectations is past experience of the suite itself, on previous occasions of audition, and memories retained of that on some level. Such memories clearly make the opening of the Polonaise both less surprising and more comprehensible than it would be for a first time auditor.[4]

Consider more closely the hearing of and reaction to the initial event of the Polonaise, which for present purposes we may take to be its first measure. The listener's reaction to this bit is notably affected, as I said,

2. In discussions of the experience of pieces of music from here on it should be assumed, unless otherwise noted, that we have to do with a listener with some previous exposure to the piece, on the order of two or three earlier hearings.
3. Alternatively, it may be triggered by onset of the music itself.
4. I leave aside the obvious broad effect of having heard tonal music of any sort before.

Figure 1. J. S. Bach, Orchestral Suite No. 2 in b minor, Polionaise

by his expectations for Baroque dance movements in general and by his memory of the bit itself from earlier auditions, as well as by norms of tonal music generally. However, the reaction to this initial event is also conditioned by the listener's memories, however subliminal, of the remainder of the Polonaise to come. Given that the listener has registered at some level how the rest of the piece will proceed, his reception of the initial event will naturally be colored by this in various ways. A prominent

Figure 1. *Continued*

feature of the Polonaise's opening event is a dotted rhythm motif of four notes that in fact permeates the entire Polonaise. And the melody of the A section of the Polonaise turns up as the bass of the B section, or "Double," whose melody is, in turn, a florid variation on the original A section melody.

Thus, to one who has heard the piece before with attention, the opening measure of the Polonaise seems not just an acquaintance encountered previously, but an event imbued with the whole of what is to follow. That is to say, a third-time auditor hears the opening as the veritable kernel of the piece, ready to germinate into various forms of itself. And his satisfaction with that first measure is thus presumably enhanced as a result. This effect on the experience of the opening is thus clearly owing to parts of the piece at some temporal distance from the opening, ones whose advent is at some level foreseen, in virtue of the piece's retention in memory.

Focus now on the point in the middle of the A section after the first complete phrase, four measures cadencing on D, has been heard twice, and a second phrase, ending on the dominant of b, has been heard once. The listener's expectations for the third phrase will be a product of at least four things: (1) internalized knowledge of how pieces of a certain sort are likely to continue, that is, of stylistic probabilities; (2) innate psychological tendencies to regard certain continuations as more likely than others; (3) stored representation of the remainder of the piece from earlier auditions; and (4) memories, more or less vivid, of what has been heard earlier in the piece on the present occasion.[5]

It is this latter element that I am interested in at the moment. Even though at this juncture the first phrase of the Polonaise is no longer a vivid memory—that is, it is not being quasi-heard at that point—it doubtless influences the listener's expectations as to the phrases that will follow, and conditions the reaction to them when they do. The third phrase begins as did the first, but then diverges in its second measure, continuing along to a cadence in b minor. It is only against the background memory of phrase one that phrase three seems at the outset a highly probably continuant, and then shortly after, a satisfyingly divergent one—satisfying in part because it returns the piece to b minor, conforming to an expectation, or tacitly gauged probability, on a higher level, deriving from an internalized norm for simple binary dance movements.

Consider, finally, the point just after the the "Double" has been heard. The A section then returns, and the listener experiences the satisfaction

---

5. Much of this tally follows the account of a listener's processing of music given in Meyer's "Music and Information Theory" and "On Rehearing Music," both in *Music, the Arts, and Ideas.*

of coming home to a familiar clime. Clearly this sensation is due to remembrance of the A section, whether or not the listener consciously realizes the repetition or reflects on it.

All of the foregoing is, one hopes, evident enough. Having heard and registered the later parts of a piece on a previous audition, and having heard and registered the earlier parts of a piece in the course of the present audition, manifestly affect the way a current part will be experienced. What one has already heard of a piece, whether on a prior occasion or the present one, is bound to influence one's present perception of any given part of that piece. This effect occurs in virtue of memory of previously heard parts, whether as a subliminal representation with which present events are compared or as an acquired tendency to respond in certain ways, against which memory present events make their appearance. The causal influence of the whole of a composition on the experience of individual parts, insofar as that whole is retained in the memory of a listener who has heard it, is not something a concatenationist can wish to dispute. That a piece is structured in such-and-such a large-scale fashion invariably has consequences for the character of the parts as sequentially heard, in virtue of the operation of memory in one guise or another.

That much must be granted. Yet, some recent experiments on the processing of music by reasonably practiced, if not expert, listeners suggests that one can easily overestimate the extent even of the *causal* relevance of large-scale form for the experience of music of such listeners.[6] It appears, for example, that most such listeners will fail to find short pieces of tonal music, ones not much longer than the Polonaise discussed above, more unified or more complete when they end in their tonic key as written, rather than in some other key, courtesy of minimal rewriting of the music by the experimenter. Now sameness of key between the beginning and ending of a piece is obviously a feature—a relatively simple one—of large-scale form. So it seems that merely possessing a large-scale form of a sort that would seem, a priori, to contribute to unity does not

---

6. The experiments, which were conducted by Nicholas Cook, are reported in the essays "The Perception of Large-Scale Tonal Closure" and "Musical Form and the Listener." The results are discussed further in chap. 1 of Cook's *Music, Imagination, and Culture.*

always conduce to a piece's being experienced as more unified or complete.[7]

Be that as it may, I am prepared to waive the question of the degree of causal influence large-scale structural relations of different sorts will have in different circumstances, in order to focus narrowly on the issue of the *appreciative* relevance of such formal aspects as grasped in conscious reflection. The question I want to highlight is not what large-scale structural relations are causally relevant to a listener's resulting experience of music, and in what degree, but rather what role, if any, does deliberate attention to large-scale form on a listener's part play in generating understanding of music as heard? In much of what follows, I am happy to assume there is some causal relevance to many aspects of large-scale form—or at least, for some significant fraction of musically sensitive listeners—because my primary concern is, rather, the appreciative relevance of bringing such aspects to reflective awareness.

### Challenges to Concatenationism: Prospective Review

As we have just noted, the organization of a piece as a whole can hardly fail to have some consequences for its aural reception, can hardly be without effect on how its parts are experienced. So it is no aim of concatenationism to deny that. What is targeted for denial is rather an undue importance placed on the whole and its intellectual apprehension from an appreciative, and subsequently, evaluative, point of view.

Yet it must be allowed that powerful considerations confront concatenationism on its proper terrain and militate against its adequacy as an account of what is appreciatively and and experientially fundamental in musical comprehension. I here draw up a list of what strike me as the primary challenges facing concatenationism. Most of the remainder of this book will be occupied in examining these challenges and

---

7. As Cook puts it in "The Perception of Large-Scale Tonal Closure," "theories that explain the organization of Classical and Romantic compositions in terms of large-scale tonal structure may not correspond in any direct manner to the perception of such music" (p. 204).

attempting to come to terms with them, either by rebuttal or by accommodation.

1. Conscious awareness of or reflection on *large-scale relationships* generally—those that fall outside the range of quasi-hearing—can affect the experience of the bit of music then being heard, modifying its perceived character, interest, or degree of connectedness to its surrounding. That is to say, such awareness importantly influences the nature of local, moment-to-moment experience of music.

2. Conscious awareness of or reflection on a piece's *formal pattern or structural type*—sonata, fugue, variations, rondo—can affect the experience of the bit of music then being heard, modifying its perceived character, interest, or degree of connectedness to its surrounding. That is to say, such awareness importantly influences the nature of local, moment-to-moment experience of music.

3. Conscious awareness of or reflection on large-scale relationships can affect the perceived *cogency or rightness* of a given succession of bit on bit, or transition from part to part.

4. Conscious awareness of or reflection on large-scale relationships, either before or during listening, can *facilitate or augment* the experience of quasi-hearing; that is, the achievement of aural synthesis of music on the local level.

5. Conscious awareness of or reflection on certain aspects of large-scale form is required for the apprehension of certain *higher-order aesthetic properties* of music.

6. Conscious awareness of or reflection on aspects of large-scale form, either during or after listening, affords a distinct *intellectual musical satisfaction* in its own right.

This list then, marks out the issues with which we will mainly be concerned. At the end of my deliberations I will return explicitly to this bill of affairs, in order to dress the balance. I will attempt to deal with these challenges in roughly the order given, but owing to the degree of interpenetration among them, it will prove almost impossible, especially at the outset, to keep the boundaries of discussion airtight. There is some artificiality, in particular, in separating off 3 from 1 and 2, since, as Gurney insists, the phenomenon of the coherence of the smallest intelligible bits of music is basically continuous with that of the cogent sequencing of more substantial musical segments, and shades into it at its outer limits. Even 4 has a way of sliding confusingly toward 1 and 2 if one is less than vigilant. At any rate, my focus will at first be challenges 1 and 2, the latter being in effect a complex subcase of the former. I will then proceed, after a pause for taking stock, to the remaining challenges, 3 through 6.

# chapter five

# LARGE-SCALE RELATIONSHIPS
# IN MUSIC

. . . the significance of a musical event—be it a tone, a motive, a phrase, or a section—lies in the fact that it leads the practiced listener to expect, consciously or unconsciously, the arrival of a subsequent event. . . .
—Leonard Meyer, *Music, the Arts, and Ideas*

Let us then begin to assess whether explicit awareness of musical architecture—or of anything beyond the musical present, broadly understood—plays a significant role in the experience of listening to music comprehendingly. Is it imperative, in particular, to focus on or attend to anything outside the span of quasi-hearing—that is, to engage in large-scale awareness or contemplation—in order basically to understand a piece of music? The simplest phenomenon of this sort is that in which in the course of listening, some bit or passage currently being heard recalls another bit or passage, from earlier in a piece, leading a listener to recognize the connection involved and contemplate it as such.

An example is afforded by the Bach Polonaise discussed earlier. In the middle section—the "Double"—the bass underneath the highly ornamented soprano line is identical with the original melody of the Polonaise, a fact of which one may very well become aware on perhaps a second or third hearing.[1] A similar opportunity offers itself in the

1. This case may seem to fall within the span of quasi-hearing, since the Double begins straight upon the Polonaise's close, in measure 12. But note that it is the initial part of the Polonaise that sounds as the Double begins, and that will not have been heard in the immediately preceding measures with which the Polonaise concludes. So there is, at that point, scope for intellectual recall of the Polonaise theme and identification of that theme with what one is then hearing in the bass.

exposition of the first movement of Haydn's Piano Sonata No. 60 in C, when after the expected modulation to G, the second subject, consisting of some running scale figures, enters over a bass that is effectively the first half of the first subject.

A third example, involving similarity rather than strict identity, is the relatedness of the opening motive of the scherzo movement (*Assez vif*) of Ravel's String Quartet in F to the sensuous d minor theme of the first movement (figure 2). A decided resemblance between them, certainly no accident, is readily apparent; for one thing, both begin with a rise of a fifth followed by a descent and quick ascent to the same note. The scherzo motive comes across, in effect, as a quickened and staccato version of the first movement theme.

In such cases as these, we often find ourselves thinking of an earlier part of a piece while auditing a present part, and explicitly cognizing the relation between the two, but without quasi-hearing the stretch of music connecting them. Let that be granted. What is in question is rather the *role* of those kinds of cognitions. How significant are their effects on us as we listen? To what extent are such awarenesses requisite to musical understanding? And what measure of satisfaction do they in themselves afford us? If we fail to achieve such awarenesses, are we cut off from basically comprehending music, and from receiving the enjoyment that usually flows from that?

One might be inclined to say that in becoming reflectively aware of similarities or identities between parts of a piece separated by more than a quasi-hearable span, one is in some sense coming to understand the piece. For one is indeed learning something about the piece, about the relationships that characterize it, or are part of its texture or fabric.

But another perspective seems defensible. It is this. What one is primarily coming to understand is not so much the *piece* itself—that is, how it moves and develops and what it conveys as it does so—but rather, something about the piece's *construction*. That is to say, the understanding that reflective awareness of a large-span musical relationship gives might be said to be first and foremost an understanding of part of how a piece works as it does, of how it appears to have been put together.[2] This is,

---

2. A natural default assumption is that musical relationships that contribute to a work's musical success have been intentionally brought about, or at least subsequently approved, by the work's creator, but such an assumption is clearly often belied in particular cases.

in turn, sometimes partially explanatory of why it gives rise to the experience that it does, for the large-scale architecture of a composition is causally relevant, as I acknowledged in Chapter 4, to the generation of its experiential content for a listener. In any event, what I am suggesting is that a grasp of relations that present parts bear to distant parts in a musical work might be seen not so much as a grasp of what the work *is* for a listener, as a grasp of how the work *works* on a listener.

An obvious rejoinder to this line of thought—that a grasp of large-span relationships constitutes a grasp of part of a piece's structure, but not of the piece per se—is this: The structure of a piece is clearly an aspect of the piece, so in grasping that structure one is, it seems, a fortiori grasping the piece as well—at least in part.

This rejoinder has merit, but there is a response to it in turn. It is that there still remains a more restricted notion of grasping a piece, one not involving conscious apprehension of large-scale relationships, which one can hold to be the fundamental notion of what it is to grasp music by ear. Such grasp would be more or less equivalent to basic musical understanding as delineated earlier. If we agree to construe grasp of a *piece* as the having of basic musical understanding with respect to it, then we may with some reason suggest that the sort of grasp that involves large-scale awareness, as basic musical understanding does not, is rightly conceived of as a grasp of something else—namely, the piece's formal *structure*.

A piece's formal structure obviously has much to do with making it what it is, and with accounting for its effectiveness, but it is not to be identified with the piece itself. There is a distinctness of objects— the piece, as opposed to the piece's formal structure—that can be taken to parallel a distinctness of understandings—basic musical understanding, on the one hand, and formal musical understanding, on the other.

By a piece's formal structure I here mean its contemplatable internal relationships of broad span, ones of similarity, identity, contrast, and the like, taken either individually or collectively, and not its small-scale, almost inarticulable, note-to-note and phrase-to-phrase connectedness. That, of course, is formal structure in *another* sense, and is in a way the most direct object of basic musical understanding. In grasping a piece one is pari passu grasping its structure in *that* sense: one is grasping,

(first movement)

Figure 2.  Ravel, String Quartet in F (excerpts)

(second movement)

**Assez vif _ Très rythmé** ($\textbf{\textit{d.}} = \textbf{92}$)

violin 1

violin 2

viola

cello

Figure 2. *Continued*

implicitly, how its smallest perceivable parts are linked or woven together. If anything of a structural order is to be identified with the piece itself, then, it is its small-scale, chainlike formedness, not its large-scale, architectural form.

To sustain this somewhat contentious distinction—between understanding a piece, on a primary and experiential level, and understanding a piece's formal structure, on a secondary and intellectual level—is one of the implicit concerns of this book.

. . .

Possibly the most important aspect of music that would appear to be placed in jeopardy, were a listener to lend no attention to a piece's large-scale relationships and overarching patterns, is its *aesthetic character or content*. For aesthetic content—by which I intend the totality of a work's aesthetic properties—is commonly held to rest on such relationships and patterns to a large degree. There are crucial aesthetic features of a composition, it might be said, to which one has no access without reflecting on relations between distant and currently experienced parts of a piece, without consciously bringing large-scale connections into focus, so that even if one could achieve some kind of comprehension of the music without engaging in cognitive activity of that sort, one would be missing a significant portion of the piece's aesthetic content. This is a serious worry, and I devote a chapter later on to systematic consideration of it (Chapter 8). In advance, though, it will be salutary to consider one such aesthetic feature, just to show that matters are by no means hopeless in this regard.

A particularly important aesthetic quality, one for whose perception large-scale awareness might seem absolutely necessary, is *unity* or *coherence*.[3] The connections between parts of extended compositions (by Bach, Haydn, Ravel) noted earlier very likely make those com-

3. Monroe Beardsley, in his classic *Aesthetics: Problems in the Philosophy of Criticism*, sees unity as a broader notion than coherence, and takes it to include the latter. According to Beardsley, unity has two components, coherence and completeness. Assuming that that distinction can be made, in the present discussion I will be regarding unity mainly under its aspect of coherence, and so equating the respective terms. Something like the completeness aspect of unity, if we follow Beardsley in this regard, will come to the fore in Chapter 8, when we deal with cases of other higher-order aesthetic properties and with the issue of intellectual pleasure in global form.

positions in some measure more coherent and unified for a listener than they would otherwise be, despite the fact that the parts in question are not aural neighbors. But that result can largely be accounted for, it seems, in terms of the effects that simply having heard and registered earlier parts of a piece can have on the experience of later parts.

The scherzo theme in the Ravel quartet, for instance, is especially gratifying because one hears it as a variant of the first movement theme, or at any rate, registers its subtle similarity to the earlier theme as retained in memory. But the earlier episode need not be consciously recollected, it seems, for this enhancement of the later episode to occur. The sense of unity—of oneness, or sameness-in-difference—arises, I claim, without explicit comparative or relational thought. A composition such as Ravel's quartet is experienced as unified because it has been constituted so as to provide that experience for a properly attuned listener, who processes the parts of a composition, as he must, sequentially, but without necessarily consciously apprehending in the musical sequence the abstract relations that it embodies or contains.

The experience of unity or coherence I am invoking has as its basic content the sense that a passage currently being heard fits with and shares something with those that have preceded it, that in coming where and when it does, a given passage in a strong sense continues, as opposed to just succeeds, what has transpired up to that point. So construed, it is clear that the crucial experience of unity in a piece of music is one that can be had as the piece proceeds, without either intellectual grasp of widely separated parts or explicit conception of the whole. Certainly apprehension, in a single imaginative-recollective act, of all the temporal parts of composition in all their interrelations is largely a phantasm of the architectonicist's mind, and the unity, if one wants to call it that, that is recordable in such an act is not the same as the unity appreciable by an involved listener in a developing stream of music.

The unity that I am concerned with here, unity of a phenomenologically manifest sort, is of course highly correlated with and dependent on certain large-scale formal characteristics—for instance, the degree of a composition's monothematicity—but it is not identical with any such characteristic.[4] Underlying relations, such as that between the themes in Ravel's quartet, clearly ground many of the perceived qualities of a musical work. But conscious awareness of these underlying relations seems unnecessary in order for a piece of music to be perceived as unified by a listener. It is not clear, further, that such awareness even augments the sense of unity a listener receives from a composition while listening. The aural coherence of music is partly explained by such connections, and thus to become aware of them is to understand more fully the basis of musical effectiveness, but the awareness as such does not obviously enhance this aural coherence to any significant degree.

If I am right, then, listeners have at individual points in the course of a piece as it progresses experiences in which the proper unity or coherence of a musical work, to the degree it has any, is manifested. It thus appears that thought on parts of a piece distant from what one is currently hearing is not required in order for a piece to evidence its unity or coherence to a listener. So, at any rate, as regards this one very important aspect of aesthetic content, it is not at all clear that access to it requires large-scale reflection of any sort.

. . .

Yet it is plain that conscious realizations of thematic or structural relationships, as might occur to a listener auditing the pieces mentioned earlier, do commonly provide a certain distinct pleasure. So what sort of pleasure is this, and what does it derive from?

4. It may help here to distinguish three sorts of unity in music: (*a*) paper unity—mere repetitions or resemblances demonstrable in a score; (*b*) monothematic structure—repetitions or resemblances hearable through normal attention; and (*c*) phenomenological unity or coherence—a sense conveyed of being unified, of fitting together or evolving organically, at any given point. Now, monothematic structure (*b*) is usually present when there is paper unity (*a*), but not always. Similarly, coherence (*c*) is usually the outcome of monothematic structure (*b*), but it seems (*c*) does not necessarily result whenever (*b*) is present.

Peter Kivy has argued, in my view unconvincingly, that unity in music is just equivalent to monothematic structure. (See his *Speaking of Art*, Chap. 1.) Leonard Meyer, on the other hand, appears to hold that motivic resemblances in music, even to the point of monothematicity, are not sufficient for musical unity. (See his *Explaining Music*, Chap. 3.) For some other discussions of unity in music and how it relates to its structural underpinnings, see R. A. Sharpe, "Two Forms of Unity in Music," and Stephen Davies, "Attributing Significance to Unobvious Musical Relationships." Both Sharpe's and Davies's perspectives on the issue are, like Meyer's, closer to my own than is Kivy's.

I suggest that, most often, this pleasure is a pleasure taken not in the relationship per se, whatever that might mean, but in what is in effect cleverness—both the composer's and one's own. We take pleasure in the composer's cleverness for having constructed his or her music so ingeniously, and in our own for having detected that construction. We delight at uncovering the hidden springs of the mechanism that has been working on us so effectively, if surreptitiously. We admire the ingenuity and craftsmanship of the maker, and we are also, it must be said, pleased with ourselves for having descried them.

Shall we say that such pleasure—which may occur, incidentally, either in the course of listening or subsequently—is not specifically musical? That would be too strong. It seems fair to say, however, that pleasure of this sort, deriving from knowledge of the causes of musical effects or impressions, must surely be secondary to pleasure in those effects and impressions themselves. That is to say, satisfaction in the expressiveness of a passage or in its urgency of motion, for example, is surely more central to music listening than satisfaction that derives from explicitly appprehending a relation the passage bears to some earlier passage that in part explains why the passage sounds or feels the way it does. Empirically such second-order pleasures of realization show themselves to be considerably less intense than the pleasures of first-order apprehension of musical substance itself. They furthermore seem parasitic on the latter in a peculiar way, in that one takes proportionally more satisfaction in detecting the basis of a particularly rewarding musical effect than in detecting the basis of a less rewarding one.

Consider another example, involving a particularly effective large-span resemblance relation. At the very end of Brahms's Third Symphony the powerful falling fourths that open the first movement return, in a peaceful and subdued guise, to close out the work (figure 3). There is a great sense of completion, rightness, and unity in this ending for an attuned listener. But this impression is not dependent, I claim, on conscious recollection of the opening statement. One can have musical understanding of this ending without conscious awareness carrying to anything outside it. If explicit recollection of the opening does occur, one may then understand, at least in part, why the ending is as satisfying as it is, but the satisfyingness of the ending itself is not obviously increased. To

Figure 3. Brahms, Symphony No. 3 in F (excerpts)

be sure, there is intellectual satisfaction in knowing how things work, and a properly aesthetic satisfaction, even, in contemplating the structural bases of effects known experientially.[5] But satisfactions such as these are arguably both not essential to basic musical understanding and relatively minor in comparison to the satisfactions inherent in basic musical understanding itself.

5. See my "What Is Aesthetic Pleasure?" in *The Pleasures of Aesthetics*.

(fourth movement, close)

*301*

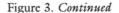

Figure 3. *Continued*

Suppose we were to grant the activity of thinking of perceptually remote parts of a piece while auditing present ones greater importance in musical experience than we have so far done. One of Gurney's observations makes any such admission less of a departure from concatenationism than it might seem. It is that even when a currently heard bit owes its effectiveness in part to some distant bit dimly recollected, the focus of attention is typically still the current bit, and not the relation between the two bits as such (that is, an aspect of large-scale form).[6] In other words, acknowledging the contribution certain wide-range awarenesses may make to musical comprehension need not amount to giving up the idea of such comprehension as essentially a matter of grasping individual successive bits and transitions between them. For in the examples we have been considering it could be argued that awareness of the distant bit functions primarily to heighten grasp of the current bit—as opposed to bringing an element of abstract form, to wit, the relation between the bits, before the mind for contemplation.

Consider another example. At the close of the second (Intermezzo) movement of Schumann's Piano Concerto, one hears twice a clear echo of the main theme of the first movement (figure 4). The resemblance is as strong as can be, and is usually remarked by an alert listener. Such a listener no doubt experiences the concerto as particularly unified at that point, and perhaps has a quantum of satisfaction in explicitly recollecting a theme encountered earlier. But it seems plausible that attention remains focused on the join being effected between the movement just ended and that about to begin, rather than carrying to a comparison between the present passage and the initial statement of the first movement's theme.

There are further points to be made. In Schumann's piece, as in the pieces by Ravel and Brahms recalled above, when conscious recognition of connection between a current bit and some earlier component of the piece saliently occurs, what exactly is the content of such a recognition? The answer, I think, is that such content is of an almost completely *nonspecific* sort. That is, the content is on the order of: "This bit, or something like it, occurred earlier." A recognition with *specific* content, by contrast, would be one that contained a more precise judgment as to where or when the present bit had been previously heard; for example: "This bit is the same as or resembles the passage concluding the development section in the preceding movement." Not only is it the rule for such recognitions in even experienced listeners to be in this sense nonspecific, rather than specific, but they need be no more than that in order to heighten a listener's sense of a piece's unity, or to pro-

6. See the long quotation from Gurney in Chapter 1 beginning ". . . the all-importance of the parts . . ."

vide the ancillary pleasures of detecting construction that were noted earlier.[7]

If I am right in holding both that nonspecific conscious recognitions and not specific ones are the rule, and that it is these that are largely responsible for any enhancement of the experience of understanding music beyond the central aural grasp of music in its moment-to-moment progression, then not much is being conceded to architectonicism. For in these cases of recalling some previously heard part, not only is the focus always on the currently heard part, instead of on the two equally, but there may be no notion of where, exactly, the earlier part figured in the preceding music, at how many places, and at what distances. That is to say, one may have no grasp of the relation between the current event and any particular, localized earlier event or events in the context of the whole span of the piece up to that point. Thus one is hardly aware of an aspect of overall structure at all, in that one does not in any very determinate way relate present to past events. Listeners in such cases standardly think only something tantamount to "What I now hear I heard before," which is by itself sufficient for the mild enhancement of experience admitted above. But surely reflective recognitions on that level can be said to represent little, if any, grasp of large-scale structure.

Let us return to the Schumann concerto. If conscious recognition of the passage at the end of the Intermezzo enhances a listener's basic comprehension of the piece, then just nonspecific recognition suffices. It is not necessary to recollect, say, that the present theme initially occurs in the first movement, in the woodwinds, after an arresting opening flourish by the piano. It is enough to recall it as familiar from some previous encounter, and this recognition can hardly count as much in the way of awareness of architectonic relations.

I come now to an additional point, one that Schumann's concerto is, again, particularly well suited to illustrate. At the passage in question, the earlier theme is not just reprised for its own sake. Schumann

7. Compare this observation of Cook's: "Unless they have both the training and the inclination to track the form of a piece of music in theoretical terms as they listen, people experience recurrence without actually observing what it is that recurs" (*Music, Imagination, and Culture*, p. 68).

(first movement)

Figure 4. Schumann, Piano Concerto in a minor (excerpts)

Figure 4. *Continued*

rather brings it back precisely in order to draw attention perceptually to the relation between this theme and the rondo theme, by letting one hear their resemblance through juxtaposing them, and by partly transforming the one into the other before one's ears in the course of launching the rondo. The whole connection is thus made manifest to the listener within the span of quasi-hearing; long-range recollective activity is here shown to be unnecessary, and of at best secondary importance. The effectiveness of this famous passage is due not to any recollective contemplation it induces on determinate relations the passage bears to particular passages that occur earlier, but rather to

(second movement, close)

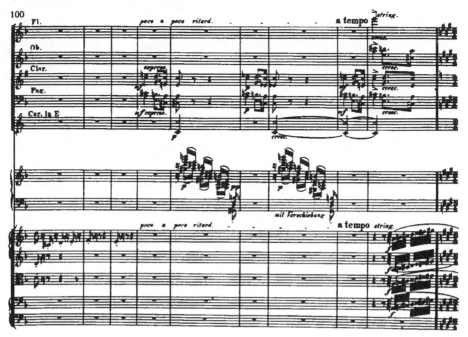

(third movement)

Figure 4. *Continued*

its making a thematic connection aurally manifest to us in the course of a cogent musical progression spanning only a few measures. Much the same could be said, to cite one other instance, of the amusing passage at the start of the finale of Beethoven's First Symphony, which doles the movement's principal theme out in small doses, at a lethargic pace, suddenly accelerating it up to speed in the sixth measure. As soon as one hears the tune at its proper, intended tempo, the connection to the preceding, halting measures is aurally grasped in vivid, as opposed to intellectual, retrospect.[8]

. . .

Let me sum up my observations in this chapter. I have allowed that explicit awareness of large-scale relationships, involving active attention to matters outside the span of quasi-hearing, occurs often enough to an engrossed listener, sometimes without being sought. I have further allowed that such awarenesses might be thought to constitute part of musical understanding, to contribute to the perception in music of aesthetic qualities, and to provide on their own account a measure of musical enjoyment. But I have tried to show that insofar as these observations exemplify certain of the challenges to concatenationism formulated earlier, they are less damaging to that position than they initially seem.

I suggested, first, that the understanding represented by large-scale formal awarenessess in music listening arguably does not belong to that basic understanding of music for which a set of identifying marks was provided earlier, and that such understanding could reasonably be maintained to have essentially a different object—the formal structure of a piece, rather than the piece, a hearable stretch of music, itself. I suggested, second, that explicit awareness of musical expanses of large extent was not clearly indispensable even to apprehension of an aesthetic quality

---

8. Recall the stress placed by Tovey on transparently developed musical relationships in the practice of the best composers, when it was their artistic aim to draw attention to such relationships. He was explicitly skeptical of the importance of the contrary procedure, as the following shows: "for instance, I shall never believe that Beethoven intended the transition passage to B flat in the first movement of the Ninth Symphony to foreshadow the choral finale which comes three-quarters of an hour afterwards. If he had meant anything by the resemblance, he could have made his meaning clear in the introduction to the finale, where he calls up the ghosts of the previous movements" ("Some Aspects of Beethoven's Art-Forms," quoted in Kerman, "Tovey's Beethoven").

such as musical unity or coherence—that the experience of a piece's coherence might, on the contrary, be contained in the character of experiences of successive parts in their given arrangement. I suggested, third, that the enjoyment derived from conscious recognition of structural relationships was of a different order from the enjoyment bound up with the basic aural involvement in or following of music—that it was parasitic on and standardly less intense than pleasure of the sort consequent on aural involvement. And I suggested, finally, that insofar as large-scale awarenesses seem implicated in the aural grasp of music—that is, insofar as they appear to have a perceptual impact on the listener in the course of listening—they are generally of such an indefinite nature as to concede little to architectonicism.

# chapter six

# SONATA AND OTHER FORMS

Anyone who picks up a book on sonata form very likely thinks he already knows what it is; and he is probably right.

—Charles Rosen, *Sonata Forms*

In the preceding chapter we pondered the nature and effects of apprehensions of music in which a currently heard part is consciously perceived in relation to some recollected but not aurally present part. Let us now consider the apprehension of large-scale forms per se, in which many or all of the parts of a piece are related to one another. In other words, what of rondo, fugue, minuet-and-trio, chaconne, variation-form, and all the rest? What role does apprehension of them play in the understanding of music?

## Sonata Form

Generally speaking, what does conscious contemplation of sonata form contribute to listening experience, and what effect does it have on the reception of individual parts? The principal question to be faced is whether having explicit awareness of a movement's sonata form during audition is crucial to auditing it successfully—to achieving basic musical understanding. Must one hear a sonata movement as such in order basically to understand it?

Before we can answer that question, however, a distinction crucial to the defense of concatenationism must be made. This is a distinction between two senses of "hearing as a sonata." One might call these, respectively, the *intellectual* and the *perceptual* senses of "hearing as a sonata." In the first sense, hearing a movement as a sonata involves entertaining certain concepts in thought and relating them to current perceptions, or consciously organizing what one is perceiving under certain articulate categories. In the second sense, hearing as a sonata involves not conscious thought or categorization but a disposition to register and respond to the musical progression one is presented with in a certain way. Thus, in terms of ideas developed earlier, hearing as a sonata in this second sense would be an aspect of the basic musical understanding that a listener might have of pieces in sonata form.

Intellectual hearing-as-a-sonata is characterized by having ideas such as exposition, bridge passage, modulation, second theme, recapitulation, and the like in the front of one's mind and applying them appropriately to musical events as they develop. Perceptual hearing-as-a-sonata, by contrast, is characterized by having certain expectations as to the course of musical events and certain attendant reactions to those events when they occur—for example, a reaction of surprise when a recapitulation structurally due and harmonically prepared for fails to turn up—and independently of what thoughts or concepts are explicitly in mind. Intellectual hearing-as is largely a matter of activated knowledge-that; for example, knowing that one has just heard the exposition section close in the dominant key. Perceptual hearing-as is not a matter of propositional knowledge at all, but is instead a matter of experiencing music in a certain manner–the activation of a kind of knowing-how.[1]

One who perceptually hears-as-a-sonata has internalized a certain norm for pieces of a given kind, and implicitly senses convergence with and divergence from that norm as presented by a particular composition. This sort of internalization does not presuppose prior abstract grasp of sonata structure. It is supplied, rather, by familiarity through listening with many actual examples of sonata movements. Typically the perceptual category—one's internalization of sonata "norm"—comes into play in an automatic manner when one encounters a piece with initial features similar enough to those possessed by the "norm."[2] On the other hand,

1. For more on this distinction, and an application to audition of the first movement of Bruckner's Fourth Symphony, see my "Musical Literacy."
2. Though one may also sometimes consciously initiate a certain mode of listening by a thought of the sort "Listen against the background of pieces X, Y, and Z," doing so does not require articulate grasp of the common features or style of X, Y, and Z.

a listener can bring the intellectual category of sonata form to bear on his hearing of a sonata movement—identifying sections as they begin and end, labeling changes of key as they occur, and so on—without perceptually hearing the piece as a sonata; that is to say, without any internalized repertoire of responses deriving from past experience of and close attention to other sonata movements.[3]

It should be no surprise, then, that my answer to the problem posed a few paragraphs back is that to audit a sonata movement successfully, one must hear it as such in the perceptual sense, though not in the intellectual one. Why is intellectual hearing-as-a-sonata—that is, conscious awareness of one sort of large-scale structure—not requisite to comprehending listening? Because, first, comprehending sonata listening is essentially listening characterized by locally coherent experience, in which one follows what is going on at each moment, connecting bits to neighboring ones through quasi-hearing, and responding appropriately to the musical motion and gesture there apprehended, and second, locally coherent experience is clearly achievable in such cases without any conscious awareness of sonata structure per se.

An analogy: If one is out in familiar country, one might be said to know the terrain, and know it quite well, even though one is ignorant, consciously, of the structure of the terrain as a whole or has never visualized it in imagination. One's knowing the terrain comes through, in such a case, in terms of one's sense of knowing "where one is" and "where one has been," and of knowing—or at least having a grounded feeling for, "what comes next" in various directions. Knowing one's way around a terrain without a map, either physical or mental, is a lot like knowing one's way around a sonata movement, upon familiarization, without any explicit global apprehension of its completed shape.

. . .

Consider the first movement of Mozart's piano sonata, in D Major, K. 311 (figure 5). This piece begins naturally enough in D with a first subject of jaunty and declamatory character. The subject is basically just

---

3. The distinction urged here is basically the same as that outlined by Nicholas Cook in the following: "hearing a piece as a sonata means hearing everything that happens in it in the light of its larger tonal context; a reflective awareness of the manner in which the music is organized need not necessarily be involved at all. And conversely, a listener might be able to tell that a piece was, as a matter of fact, a sonata, but not be able to hear it as one" (*Music, Imagination, and Culture,* p. 51).

Figure 5. Mozart, Piano Sonata in D, K. 311, 1st movement

Figure 5. *Continued*

Figure 5. *Continued*

Figure 5. *Continued*

Figure 5. *Continued*

Figure 5. *Continued*

scales and turns, but with an ear-catching appoggiatura ending to the first phrase in measure 4. In measure 7 begins some transitional material, ending with a rapid arpeggiated alternation of the chords of D and A, leaving the latter triumphant. The second subject begins in the dominant, A, at measure 16. Though more relaxed than the first subject, it is rather similar to it; turns, scalar figures, and appoggiaturas are also prominent here. The momentum toward a firm close in A is picked up at measure 24, with rapid sixteenth-note figuration which continues in one hand or the other until just before the end of the exposition. A third, or closing, subject is introduced at measure 28, and is distinguished from the preceding two most markedly by its initial gentle stepwise fall of three quarter notes, and a triplet ornament soon after. This is then repeated, leading precipitately to an apparent conclusion at measure 37, a loud full cadence on A. But that is followed, almost shyly, by the exposition's real close (measures 38-39): another affirmation of A, this time *piano*, passing by an appoggiatura chord on the penultimate beat.

The development starts out in e minor with the closing figure of the exposition cleverly combined with a figure from the third measure of the second subject. After this is restated in D, the music plunges into a stormy excursion in b minor with further working out of the exposition closing figure, ending with some puzzling cadences in measures 56 and 57 which leave one somewhat at sea harmonically.[4] Instead of a clarifying return to the tonic, for which one has been half-prepared, a pseudo-recapitulation ensues after a half-measure rest, consisting in two presentations of the third subject in the key of G. This leads to a running passage which finally eventuates in the familar arpeggiated alternation of A and D that occurred in the exposition (measures 15 and 16). Here this serves as a dominant preparation for the return of the second subject in D major, this key now holding the stage until the end of the movement. Thus the true recapitulation commences, unusually, with the second subject (measure 78).

The rapid figuration from measure 24 recurs at measure 87. It is followed shortly by the third subject again, now in the tonic, concluding on a firm D major chord, which serves in turn as the initial stroke of the

4. This is a matter of those measures hinting, to roughly the same degree, at both continuation in D and continuation in G.

first subject which opened the sonata. After that subject is restated, there is a brilliant coda of scales and broken chords. But now, instead of the premature full cadence occurring in the exposition, Mozart substitutes a sort of deceptive cadence, on rolled chords, after which comes the gentle true close, mirroring that of the exposition.[5]

. . .

With this brief overview of the most obvious overall structure of the movement before us, we must ask to what extent a listener's comprehension of this movement depends upon conscious awareness of any aspect of the structure we have just detailed. Must a listener, for example, be consciously aware of the beginning of the development or the beginning of the recapitulation when they occur? Must she explicitly compare the recapitulation with the exposition while she is hearing the former? Must she contemplate the symmetry of the movement as a whole, with its manifest ABA' patterning?

I would say that the core experience of understanding the movement need involve none of this type of awareness. If one has locally coherent experience of the movement, I suggest, then one is hearing it with understanding: one grasps and responds appropriately to each part as it comes, connecting it to nearby bits, fore and aft, in a quasi-hearable unity. For this understanding to occur, explicit reflection on where one is at any point in the overall structure of events is unnecessary. If one is an attuned and practiced listener, one will register the temporary repose at the end of the exposition, and will have the appropriate expectations for more unsettling occurrences to follow immediately at the outset of the development, and so on, even though thought of sectional sonata structure be entirely absent.

Let us focus on some of the more important junctures in the experience of listening to this sonata. One such is the presentation of the second subject in the dominant at measure 16, announced by four unambiguous A major chords. This event seems perfectly satisfying, conformable with what has gone before, though as we know, something of a departure as well. On the other hand, were the second subject to have been introduced

---

5. It is perhaps not strictly a deceptive cadence (i.e., a V → VI), for the first chord is something more like a diminished seventh—two music analysts I consulted on its designation were not in agreement—but it functions analogously; that is to say, the first chord, however it is best described, has the effect of a dominant.

in D's relative minor—b minor—after such preparation, we would be highly disconcerted. But neither reaction entails any sort of explicit correlating of the later passage with the opening one with regard to key relation. The experience of the second subject's entrance is, to be sure, colored by all that has been heard earlier, but in comprehending listening attention can happily be confined to just the most immediate musical context—to the preceding few measures.

Or consider the pseudo-recapitulation at measure 58. The attuned listener finds this amusingly disorienting. Not only is he confronted with the subdominant after being psychologically prepared for a tonic return by the apparent winding down of development-like activity, but the subdominant appears bearing the third subject, and not the expected first subject. In order to experience this amusing disorientation a listener need not have any explicit cognizance of where she is in terms of divergence from some norm of tonal patterning. Similarly, the unusual return to the tonic with the second theme, and the rounding out of the recapitulation with the long-awaited first theme (unheard since the opening of the movement), make their effect and are comprehended without any intellectual apprehension of the formal structure, typical and atypical features alike, as a whole.

In a more regular sonata movement, such as the first movement of Mozart's Piano Sonata K. 309, in which the order of events in the recapitulation conforms exactly to that established in the exposition, the prevailing impression during the recapitulation will be one of familiarity, of a reassuring return of previously encountered material. In K. 311 a related impression—one of sameness-with-difference, to be exact—registers tellingly at the "deceptive" cadence followed by real close in the recapitulation, which clearly echoes the similar ending of the exposition. But the point is that gratifying impressions of familiarity, unity-through-change, and the like require no conscious reflection on where or when some musical material was previously encountered, no active appreciation of the pattern of events, thematic or harmonic, as a whole.

Another point of potential interest, in the recapitulation of a standard sonata movement, is the divergence between the bridge passage connecting first and second subjects in the recapitulation and the corresponding passage in the exposition. There will generally be some notable difference here in that the bridge passage in the exposition is charged with effecting a modulation, whereas the bridge in the recapitulation, though it may give the impression of harmonic movement, nevertheless holds the music to the tonic key. I do not deny that conscious comparison, while listening, between these two bridges may provide a certain analytical or intellectual satisfaction. What I do maintain is that a listener need not engage in conscious correlation in order to sense the interest of a different bridge procedure from exposition to recapitulation. A listener will experience the second bridge against her earlier experience of the first one, but she need not have the latter in mind for comprehending listening to occur. As for the additional enjoyment that conscious reflection on the contrast may provide, it is worth recalling Gurney's observation that the nature of the thought in such cases invariably places in the forefront of consciousness the current passage, not the relation between the two passages as such, and even less their places in the overall sonata scheme.

.   .   .

There is an aspect of this movement as a whole that we have heretofore overlooked. The form of the movement, on the broadest sectional level, is not strictly ABA' (or exposition/development/recapitulation), but rather AABA' (or exposition/exposition/development/recapitulation), owing to the indicated and customary repeat of the exposition. Now, it might be thought that conscious apprehension of form on this level is implicated by the fact that listeners are often sensitive to the omission of the exposition repeat in performance, to the extent of being disturbed by or even resentful of it. If a concatenationist view of basic musical understanding is correct, one might ask, what is the source of this commonly observed displeasure in an alteration in large-scale form?

We should note first that there is no problem in accounting for this phenomenon in the case of a listener who has already heard a composition a few times in the past—that is to say, the default case in our deliberations. If on those occasions the composition was heard with the repeat properly taken, then on subsequent hearings the listener, having retained some memory of the piece from past performance, will naturally expect it to proceed as before, and will be taken aback by such a large divergence from the remembered course. Apprehension of the movement as a whole would seem to be irrelevant to this reaction.

On the other hand, consider the case of a listener who has *not* previously heard the composition, and suppose he too is disturbed by a performance of it without exposition repeat. Should we conclude that here the listener is contemplating inwardly an overall ABA' pattern, and finding it aesthetically inferior to one of AABA'? Surely not, for an internalized and nonconscious expectation to the effect that the expositions of Classical sonata movements generaly repeat themselves is sufficient to explain the listener's discomfiture at one course of events rather than the other. The discomfiture arises just at the point at which developmental activity is heard instead of the expected return to the opening; it does not issue from contemplation of or reflection on large-scale proportions. It is even possible to explain, on concatenationist principles, a reaction of dissatisfaction at that point on the part of a listener who neither knows this particular piece nor has any particular expectations as to the likelihood of an exposition repeat in a Classical sonata. It might just be, for many pieces, that the beginning of the development is a more satisfying event coming after two statements of the exposition rather than one. The progression from the conclusion of exposition to the outset of development may simply be more cogent or compelling with a repeated exposition than without it.[6] Here as in other cases, it does not seem impossible to explain effects apparently due to awareness of overall form in terms instead of experiences of individual parts and transitions, in the contexts, funded by earlier perception, in which they occur.

Thus what we find in typical instances of appreciation of the features of a sonata movement, I believe, is that the reactions and satisfactions characteristic of comprehending listening are had without cognizance of overall structure or contemplation of large-scale relations. What does happen, on the contrary, is appreciation of individual parts as they occur, influenced naturally by the hearing of earlier parts, with explicit awareness

---

6. A specific explanation is actually not hard to produce in the case of sonata form. Since the development in such pieces generally commences in the dominant or some other nontonic key, the particular quality of the progression from end of exposition to beginning of development (e.g., V → V) is weakened if the listener is not given, earlier on, the contrasting progression from end of exposition to beginning of exposition (V → I), when the repeat is taken. The particular trajectory chosen by the composer at the outset of the development loses some of its effect if its implicit contrast—a return to the exposition's opening—is not aurally given.

of only a small—that is to say, quasi-hearable—stretch of music surrounding the part then being literally heard.[7]

The reader may wonder why I chose K. 311, a somewhat atypical example of Classical sonata procedure, to illustrate my claims about the processing of a sonata movement. The answer is not far to seek. The reason I chose it was precisely that it was somewhat atypical, though still recognizable as falling in the genre. It seemed that if I could account for the grasp of even an atypical sonata in concatenationist terms, merely on the basis of intent listening given a prior background of listening to related pieces, it would be obvious how such would go for pieces whose procedure more nearly conformed to expectational norms.

. . .

Now that we have a piece of music before us in some detail, and since our earlier discussion of the notion of quasi-hearing was somewhat abstract, I propose to trace the experience or process of quasi-hearing as it would be manifested in listening to the opening portion of the Mozart movement examined above. The central feature of quasi-hearing, you will recall, is the experiencing of a stretch of music *as if* one were hearing it in its entirety, while actually only hearing some bit contained within that stretch. It involves apprehending a stretch of music as a motion and yet complete, or as an almost-present whole, through the offices of vivid memory and anticipation. It is worth attempting to detail, just once, a typical train of quasi-hearing, since this phenomenon is arguably the most distinctive characteristic of comprehending listening, and by itself almost a sufficient condition of it.

The first three measures of K. 311 form a very cogent group, and are no doubt quasi-heard as a unit at any point within them by a listener familar with the piece and practiced in Classical style. The grounds of this cogency are not hard to find. Melodically, measure 1 consists essentially of

7. Cook, reflecting on experiments he and others have conducted on the listener's processing of music, arrives at similar conclusions: "a sonata form which the theorist sees as a compact, closed pyramid of formal relationships, representing progressive subdivisions of the music as a whole, was apparently experienced additively, as an open, linear sequence of discrete units. It is of course possible to instruct people on how to perceive a sonata according to the traditional categories of formal description . . . [but] even such listeners as have the requisite knowledge do not in practice listen this way except when specifically requested to do so; in other words, listening for form as defined in this manner is not a normal mode of aesthetic enjoyment" ("Musical Form and the Listener," p. 241).

an upward D-F#-(G)-A motion, outlining the tonic triad. Measure 2, with its rising A-B-C#-D, is easily heard as a continuation of the motion of measure 1. On the third beat of measure 3 occurs a turn around G identical to that on the last beat of measure 1, which unifies those measures powerfully in hearing. Measures 4 through 6 approximately repeat measures 1 through 3, and are readily heard together with them. Measure 6 eventuates smoothly in a new motive, which occupies measures 7 through 10 (and which, curiously, never reappears in the course of the movement). Under the new motive in measure 8, however, is a bass figure resembling the turns of the melody in the second half of measure 6, which thus keeps measure 6 resonant in memory while measure 8 is being heard.

Measures 11 and 12 are taken up by scalar runs that have only a slight connection with earlier melodic material, leading to some broken figures in sixteenth notes that resemble, and thus may seem familiar in virtue of, the sixteenth note turns in measures 1, 3, 4, and 6. However, very likely they are not heard *with* them. That is, one does not quasi-hear the whole first fifteen measures while hearing measures 12 through 15. One does, though, at least quasi-hear measures 1 through 5 at measure 4, measures 4 through 7 at measure 6, measures 6 through 10 at measure 8, measures 7 through 11 at measure 10, and so on. At an abrupt break, such as that at measure 16, where the second subject begins, quasi-hearing reaches back plausibly only to the preceding measure or two. The two-note rising appoggiatura motives throughout this second theme, which derive from the tail end of the opening subject (measure 4), certainly render the theme easily grasped, familiar-sounding, and pleasing in its context. But one hardly hears the second subject as forming a single whole in perception with the opening subject fifteen measures back: so one does not grasp as a single, almost present musical motion the first sixteen measures of K.311.

Thus, the vivid experience of musical material in the course of this composition is limited to stretches of rather small extent. The amount of music that will be vividly experienced at any given moment ranges from a few measures to perhaps twenty or thirty measures, depending on the quality of the connections among them and on the tempo of the passage. Phrase construction, naturally, will have a lot to do with the extent of quasi-hearing in much music, and it would be fair to say that if there is a paradigm quasi-hearable stretch, it is that occupied by a standard four-to-eight-measure phrase.

At any rate, the entire sonata movement we have been discussing—a relatively small-scaled instance of the species—is at no time the object of vivid apprehension as a whole. Rather, it is comprehended in overlapping segments that become, sequentially, the objects of vivid apprehension. There is indeed a cumulative effect of the entire sequence, and at any point in midsequence, but it is not due to experience of the whole as such.

### Prelude, Variations, and Allegretto

What has been said from a concatenationist perspective about a listener's comprehension of a sonata movement can be maintained for listening comprehension of pieces of different sorts, whether more purely processive, or more purely formal. The distinction between processive and formal organization, which I take from Leonard Meyer, is a useful one.[8] In a highly processive piece, such as the majority of preludes for keyboard from the Baroque to the Romantic period, the argument unfolds in a relatively seamless manner without significant completion or closure occurring until the very end. The music proceeds without notable discontinuity, that is to say, without shaping itself into semi-independent units along the way. The musical implications for an attuned listener at any point are a function of the entire course of the piece as a whole up to that point, though as I suggested earlier, those deriving from more proximate portions will generally have a greater impact on the listener's experience.

In a piece of largely formal character, such as a Classical theme and variations, things are rather otherwise. There is constant and regular closure throughout the composition, occurring at the end of every variation, and in many cases within variations themselves. A standard theme and variations consists evidently in a series of independent and self-contained units, and is predominantly heard as such. Although individual

8. See his *Explaining Music,* chap. 4. A related distinction is enunciated by William Newman, "Musical Form as a Generative Process," between music that is primarily based on motives and motivic development and music that is based primarily on the building up of phrases into larger units, through relations such as that of antecedent and consequent.

variations are characterized by processive development, there are by and large few implicative relationships between separate variations. The expectations generated in a listener in the middle of the fourth variation result from hearing the first half of the variation, as well as from knowledge of the original theme, but are not generally a function of what transpires in the first, second, and third variations.

A sonata movement, such as that from Mozart's K. 311, is intermediate between a highly processive and a highly formal sort of composition. Like a theme and variations, it contains sections or isolatable units, but its formal character, in the above sense, is much lessened, for two reasons. One, the units in a sonata movement exhibit a range of degrees of closure or completeness, and not all of them are so decisive and clear-cut as the regular full and half-cadences of a variation movement. Think of the development sections in many sonatas, and the subtle ways such sections can be entered on and exited from. Two, the earlier units in a sonata movement generally bear significant implicative relations to later units, and yield expectations for the train of events within those later units. An exposition section, for example, implies much for the recapitulation to come, whereas a third variation standardly implies little about the course of a fifth variation.

Let us see, then, whether the experience of listening with understanding to compositions that are either more processive or more formal than sonata movements provides any particular challenge to a concatenationist view of music. Take the C major prelude from Book 2 of the *Well-Tempered Clavier* (figure 6). Few pieces of traditional music are more purely processive than this. It develops without break or pause, without arrivals of significance, from beginning to end, notwithstanding the fact that around its twentieth measure there does occur a certain amount of transposed repetition of earlier material.

It is perhaps obvious that comprehension of highly processive pieces is readily explicable on concatenationist principles. Basic comprehension of a piece such as the C major prelude requires only an absorption in the unfolding of each measure out of the preceding one, in the development, moment to moment, of each strand in the contrapuntal fabric. The intertwining of lines or voices to create a dominant melodic movement at each point is registered by the listener without being sorted into its separate components, and recurring motives are sensed without being identified as to their exact earlier provenance. As far as large-scale form in the usual sense is concerned, there is little such to grasp in this prelude. No salient structure importantly transcends the short phrase-to-phrase connectedness of this piece, and there is thus almost nothing toward which conscious large-scale apprehension could plausibly be directed. No significant contribution to a listener's experience of the C major prelude derives from awareness of the form of the whole, such as it is.

This is not to deny that the C major prelude can be analyzed harmonically and motivically, and certain connections or implications demonstrated between widely separated events. But it is even more evident than in the case of sonata comprehension that a listener need take no explicit note of these connections or implications, and that they can hardly be said to constitute the form of the piece in any sense important for listening. The music analyst Hugo Riemann, for example, sees the prelude as falling into eight periods of roughly equal length, and traces various modulations occurring throughout, in which the subdominant and parallel minor keys figure prominently, but I am unable to connect such an analysis with my normal attentive hearing of this piece, a piece I have heard countless times.[9] I imagine that most listeners would concur.

. . .

In the case of a theme and variations, on the other hand, there unquestionably is a large-scale form—A, A′, A″, A‴, and so on—and a dominant, or at least presumptive, relationship between each variation and the original theme. Awareness of this form, however, is both dispensable to achieving intelligent listening and of no interest in itself, being a pattern of the utmost simplicity. Naturally one must hear a piece in variation form *as* a theme and variations, but one need not ever have before the mind the "beads on a string" pattern that the variations constitute as a whole. The relation of each variation to the theme need not be reflected on as such in comprehending listening. One hears each variation in the light of one's memory of the original theme and the preceding variations, especially immediately preceding ones, but one does not revive such memory for reflective comparison while listening.

There is no need to discriminate consciously between present and past variations in order to have, from a well-composed set of variations, an

9. Hugo Riemann, *Analysis of J. S. Bach's Well-Tempered Clavier,* 2:2–4.

90    *Music in the Moment*

Figure 6. J. S. Bach, Prelude in C, *Well-Tempered Clavier*, Book 2

Figure 6. *Continued*

appropriate and pleasurable apprehension of unity in variety. A listener does not silently rerun the theme while auditing each variation. Nor does he abstractly contemplate the relations obtaining between different variations, or between given variation and theme.

Instead, the listener hears each variation through the original theme, retained in memory, which theme thus acts as a kind of aural lens. When hearing a fifth variation, say, the original theme is not so much an object of attention as an influence on, a shaper and focuser of, one's perception of that variation. Attention is centered on the emerging variation, not on its abstract relationship to its generative theme.

Roger Scruton characterizes the hearing of variations as follows:

> Hearing a variation involves a particular kind of thought process. It is not sufficient—nor is it necessary—to remember the original melody while hearing its variant, nor is it sufficient to think of the variant as similar. . . . In hearing a variation we hear the variation as the original theme: we recognize the original melody in it . . . hearing the new theme as a variation is like discovering a relation between the two themes. But the peculiar feature is that this relation is something that we hear . . . we do not simply have it in mind as we listen—it comes alive in the notes themselves.[10]

A concatenationist will find little to demur with in that. As long as each variation of a set of variations is heard a certain way, that is, as a variation, in the wake of the initial theme that precedes it, proximally or distally, there is no need either for variation form as such to rear its head during comprehending listening, or for a comprehending listener to engage in explicit comparison of variation with theme or other variation.

In his discussion of Brahms's *Variations on a Theme by Handel,* Nicholas Cook observes that a number of the later variations in that set have in fact only a very tenuous connection to the theme that putatively spawns them, and in some cases are not heard in relation to the theme at all, but only in relation to immediately neighboring variations. In a remarkably concatenationist spirit, he concludes that

10. Scruton, *Art and Imagination,* pp. 178–180.

the organization of the variation set is not so much concentric—with each variation deriving coherence from its relationship to the theme—as edge-related, with each variation being lent significance by its relationship to what comes before or after it.[11]

We may still admit that, with a piece in variation form, having heard the theme first, whether or not it is consciously recalled during listening, subtly colors the hearing of even highly remote variations, if only in virtue of the most general norms, of key, theme length, and phrase structure, that the theme's initial statement sets up. But that would just be to acknowledge, once again, the potential *causal* relevance to musical experience of remote antecedents. It would not be to concede the need, so far as *appreciation* is concerned, to fix those antecedents in mental space for contemplative regard.

.  .  .

I turn now to a portion of César Franck's Symphony in d minor for a further illustration of what comprehending listening, on a basic level, does and does not require. The symphony's second movement, Allegretto, will serve us as another example of a piece of music midway between the poles of highly processive and highly formal compositions, though one that does not conform in an obvious way to a preexisting pattern such as sonata form.[12] I first offer a standard, low-level analysis of the movement, indicating its thematic and harmonic plan, and then ask whether that plan need enter the consciousness of a listener, and in what degree, for basic musical understanding to occur.

The movement opens in b-flat minor with a solemn theme ($\alpha'$) stated pizzicato in the strings (measures 1–16). This theme is followed by a full statement on English horn of the main theme proper ($\alpha$), while $\alpha'$, in effect a skeletal reduction of $\alpha$, continues underneath, along with a countermelody in the violas and cellos (measures 16–48) (see figure 7). This passage gives way to a gentle, soaring theme in B-flat major ($\beta$), with the sinuous chromatic motion typical of Franck's melodic gift (measures

11. Cook, *Music, Imagination, and Culture*, p. 64.
12. The movement combines traits of a traditional slow movement and a scherzo, and was probably so conceived by Franck. As one commentator of fifty years ago aptly remarks: "The form is difficult to define, but it is all perfectly clear to follow" (Norman Demuth, *César Franck*, pp. 82–83). I hope to demonstrate as much in my discussion.

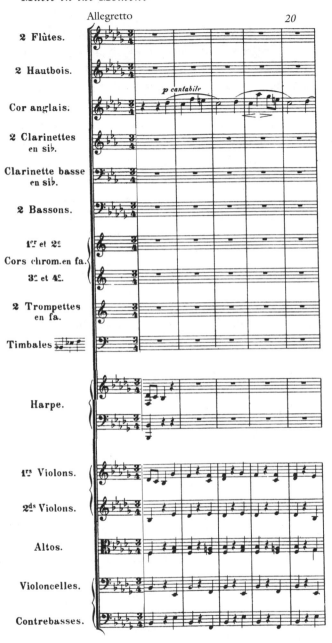

Figure 7. Franck, Symphony in d minor, 2d movement (excerpts)

Figure 7. *Continued*

Figure 7. *Continued*

Figure 7. *Continued*

Figure 7. *Continued*

Figure 7. *Continued*

49–86). After a brief reprise of α plus α′, again in b-flat minor (measures 87–95), there is a transition to the movement's scherzo section by way of preliminary scraps of the scherzo's mysterious g minor triplet theme (τ) punctuated by consoling figures vaguely reminiscent of theme β (measures 96–107). The scherzo section proper, in which g minor holds sway throughout, is taken up with the elaboration of τ, combined effectively with α′ in the bass (measures 108–145) (see figure 7).

At this point, about halfway through the movement, Franck gives us a new theme (δ), a dotted, rocking affair wholly positive in mood, in the key of E-flat major, though as chromatic as β, if not more so. The accompaniment in the second violin is in triplets, preserving a connection with τ, and a significant timpani motto (triplet plus quarter note) toward the end of this section helps bring it to a close (measures 146–184). Next there is a reprise of τ and of g minor, but soon combined with the movement's main theme, α (measures 185–210). The succeeding stretch of music returns us to b-flat minor, with α and τ in combination continuing to be the main business (measures 211–232). There is then an unheralded shift to the key of B major, under whose aegis occurs a brief reminiscence of β, followed by one of δ, and then one of β again, before δ is given a valedictory voicing in the key of D (measures 233–248). The remainder of the movement is in the nature of a coda (measures 249–273), primarily occupied with theme β, and returns the music to B-flat major—the tonic key, if altered in mode. Its closing gestures (at measures 262–270), clearly echo those of the end of the earlier B-flat major section (measures 80–86).

What, then, is the relation between what a listener who understands this movement is doing as he listens and the thematic-harmonic plan just detailed? Very little, I suggest, at least as far as conscious awareness is concerned. The comprehending listener of Franck's Allegretto, one who after a number of auditions has basic musical understanding in regard to it, is able to follow its progress in real time, to quasi-hear its phrases, melodies, and transitions, to sense its developmental implications from point to point, and to register such emotional character as it develops throughout. Such a listener responds to the music's changes with the degree of naturalness or wonder they warrant in context, while synthesizing the temporal flow aurally in such a manner as to be inside the music, able to foresee—or better, forehear—its immediate course with varying degrees of exactitude. Typically, such a listener's attainment of basic musical understanding will also be marked by some degree of reproductive or continuational ability as regards the musical fabric itself.

Thus the comprehending listener is able to take in theme $\alpha$—or at least its large first half, itself sixteen measures long—as a single utterance. Such a listener senses how fittingly $\alpha'$ serves as the accompaniment to $\alpha$ during its initial sounding on English horn—though without necessarily recognizing the structural identity between them—and registers the solemn, even lugubrious, character of the movement's initial material. The listener begins, toward the close of the opening section in b-flat minor, to expect something contrasting to ensue, and when it does—theme $\beta$ at measure 49—he connects this smoothly in quasi-hearing fashion with the music that preceded it, and recognizes a change of tonality, if only one from dark to light. Passing over all the intervening processing in this vein and moving right to the movement's close—what I have labeled its coda—a comprehending listener will of course find its material familiar and its tonality comforting, and will perhaps appreciate, through a diffuse and nonspecific recollection, its contrast in mood with the music with which the movement began.

But what of the music's architecture as such? What of the relationships brought out in garden-variety analysis, let alone those that a more searching one would reveal? Some of the movement's salient architectural features, which could be the object of intellectual cognition, are these. First, there is the progression of keys gone through (b-flat, B-flat, b-flat, g . . .), the relations of those keys to one another (e.g., parallel major), and the association of given themes with particular keys (e.g., $\tau$ and g minor). Second, there is the fact of the opening key's not returning until about three-quarters of the way through the piece. Third, there are matters of proportion, such as the ratios of lengths of various sections of the movement to one another. Fourth, there is the parallel between the close of the movement as a whole in B-flat and the close of the first B-flat section, almost two hundred measures earlier. Fifth, there is the issue of the recurrence of themes, in terms of when and where they have occurred before. And sixth, there is the overall shape of the movement as a sequence of sections thematically or harmonically defined, which could be characterized, very roughly, as a modified ABA.

Unsurprisingly, I suggest that none of this need have been grasped by a listener who nevertheless basically understands Franck's evocative tonal essay. Such a listener is sensitive to changes of key, but without knowing necessarily what they are, or if they have previously occurred, or how remote harmonically the keys involved are from one another. Such a listener notes when one section gives way to another, but without explicitly perceiving or comparing their durational proportions. Such a listener recognizes the movement's close as having been prefigured, but without necessarily recalling exactly when and where. Such a listener registers thematic recurrences, to be sure, but without placing themes in a mental landscape showing their points of first appearance, and without noting how many recurrences of a given theme there are. Such a listener does not necessarily consciously remark respects in which a given thematic occurrence differs from an earlier one, beyond noting that it is different. And finally, such a listener may have no conceptual grasp of the movement's overall shape—the ABA with modifications mentioned above—without in any way forgoing a grasp of its connectedness and expressiveness as an object of audition.

As we have had occasion to observe earlier, there is a difference between registering and responding to a feature on a perceptual level and grasping a feature on an intellectual level, through conscious thought of an articulate sort. The same feature may, indeed, be differently cognized by different listeners, or by the same listener at different times. One may, at different times, be more or less inclined toward or more or less adept at intellectual grasp of structural relationships, even fairly important ones. For instance, one might fail, in this movement of Franck's symphony, to explicitly recognize the g minor episode as itself a variation of the movement's main theme.[13] Yet one might be hearing it as a variation nonetheless, feeling the kinship to and naturalness of continuation with what precedes that episode, and be aware of something that confirms its variation status, namely, how well the new g minor tune fits with the old main theme, which persists underneath in the form of a bass. Being aware of the variation relationship in question on an articulate level is unnecessary—or so I claim—for comprehending listening of the music.

·  ·  ·

The twentieth-century composer and theorist Ernst Toch proposed a distinction between *forms,* standard patterns used over and over again

13. Indeed, this was my condition, until a more musically trained ear brought the fact to my attention.

in a tradition, and *FORM,* the principle or quality of progression, move-ment, and continuity displayed by any successful piece of music. The elevation of FORM over forms is very much in the spirit of our present discussion, as the following extracts from Toch's major treatise on musical aesthetics reveal:

> A piece may be written in any one of the classified forms to its minutest detail and still may exhibit a pitifully poor FORM. And a piece may not reveal the slightest affiliation to any of the traditional forms, and yet may be a prodigous masterpiece of FORM. . . . what else but formalism and pedantry is it if theory keeps teaching analysis of the few forms? Is it a worthy goal to the creative mind to know that this piece is written in sonata form, that in rondo form? *Who cares?* Surely not the composer. Surely not the performer. Surely not the audience.
> . . . So in a piece like [the prelude to] *Die Meistersinger,* form is neither a loose potpourri, nor just the "grouping of a given thematic material," as the notion of form is frequently defined. Irregular and unruly in every detail as it seems to be, akin nowhere in detail or *in toto* to any of the traditional forms, its form is compellingly, irresistibly, inescapably present—omnipresent, sovereign, responding in the high-est degree to *the shaping forces in music.*[14]

Whether a piece viewed as a whole is in sonata form or variation form, or else displays the more continuously unfolding development of a typical prelude, or else exemplifies a not-so-readily classified sectional form—such as that displayed by the movement of Franck just examined—is not a matter of great moment either for the listener's conscious orientation to a work or for the critic's attempt to ascertain its value as music. What is of prime importance in each case is involvement in and assessment of the work's individual mode of evolution—its FORM, if you will—as it materializes at each moment. If the prelude to *Die Meistersinger* fails to partake clearly of any antecedently recognized forms or patterns of prolongation, then, says Toch, so much the worse for them. Whatever its form in an overall, spatialized sense might be, this information turns out to be of surprisingly little importance to either the auditor or the

14. Ernst Toch, *The Shaping Forces in Music,* pp. 154, 163.

appraiser of the music, however important it may have been, heuristically, from the point of view of the composer, and however important it might be, causally, in terms of structural factors that as a matter of fact underlie the music's aural cogency for a listener without the listener's attending to or conceptualizing them as such.

Wagner's overture, we might add, is hardly unusual in the respect Toch underlines, especially as the nineteenth century gives way to the twentieth. Much the same could be said, for example, of the opening movements of Sibelius's Fourth, Fifth, and Sixth Symphonies, of Debussy's *Prélude de l'après-midi d'un faune,* or of Scriabin's *Poem of Ecstasy,* none of which displays evident reliance on preexisting large-scale formal patterns. Of course, this does not prevent such pieces from being followed understandingly, at least after a few hearings.

### Challenges to Concatenationism: Interim Assessment

It is time for a more definitive assessment of the most fundamental of the challenges to concatenationism formulated in Chapter 4, 1 and 2. Those challenges concern the bearing on a listener's musical experience of explicit awareness of individual large-scale musical relationships and of large-scale musical forms or patterns. With that assessment concluded, we will be in a position to proceed to the rest of the challenges to concatenationism formulated earlier. Focusing first on 1, we have then to consider, once more, these questions: What is the effect on the experience of an individual bit of music of awareness of a large-scale relationship in which the bit figures? To what extent does such awareness impact the character of the bit as perceived?

The observations we have already made on this score certainly suggest that such effect, such impact, is generally negligible—that architectonicist dogma on this point is, at the least, overblown. A qualm, though, might quite reasonably remain, concerning a possibility that has been only glancingly addressed in our reflections so far. Might not conscious awareness of a remote musical relationship in some cases directly augment the impressiveness of a given bit as aurally experienced? In other words, might not a bit of music very well seem better, or strike one as more fitting, on the level of basic musical understanding, in virtue of explicit attention carried then and there to some discernible large-scale relation in which the bit in question was one term?

Let us ponder this question in light of some of the cases of large-scale relationships considered earlier. Recall first the Polonaise from the Bach b minor suite. As I remarked before, at the return of the A section of this tripartite movement the attuned listener experiences the satisfaction of regaining after some time away a familiar place, owing obviously to retention in memory of the A section across the intervening B section. Given the listener's aural experience up to that point, and his attunement to the norms and limits of the style at hand, the reprise of A when it in fact occurs could hardly be more right, apt, or effective. But now suppose that the listener also reflects on or explicitly cognizes, at that moment, the overall arch form (ABA) then beginning its downward descent. Leaving for later discussion whatever distinctly intellectual delight this recognition might provide, is there here any real enhancement of the aural rightness noted above and of the aural satisfaction attendant on it? To my mind—that is to say, to the best of my introspective ability and musical sense—the answer is no. The structuring of the piece, absorbed and retained unconsciously by the attentive listener, itself suffices for the aural rightness and satisfaction in question, and does not seem susceptible to significant enhancement through explicit contemplation of such formal structure.

Move on now to Ravel's string quartet. I remarked above the underlying resemblance between the scherzo theme of the quartet's second movement and the second theme of the first movement. When our paradigmatic experienced listener confronts the beginning of this third movement, on what does the aural effectiveness and interest for him of its scherzo theme at that juncture depend? I contend that for a listener who has dutifully absorbed the quartet's preceding movement—including, in particular, the implicit preparation or foreshadowing of the scherzo theme in the d minor melody of that movement—the effectiveness and interest of the theme are assured by its own internal small-scale construction, and by its occurring when and where it does. Without that foreshadowing, it is true, the scherzo theme would probably lack some measure of contrastive piquancy with the music that precedes it. But with both factors in place—internal construction and appropriate placement— the theme's verve, excitement, and quality of self-confidence are already fully there.

Suppose, though, that the listener now adverts mentally to the conformant relation between the scherzo theme before his ears and its predecessor in the preceding movement. Does his contemplation of or attention to this relationship add anything to the effectiveness of the theme for him, on either the kinetic or the expressive level? As far as I can make out, it does not. Rather, the essential dynamism of the movement as a whole for an attuned listener appears to reside in and be entirely explicable by reference to nothing more than the character of individual bits and successions that can be contained within sequential acts of quasi-hearing. In other words, the musical gist of the movement emerges unaided for focused listening of a concatenationist sort. Conjoined awareness of conformant relations between far-flung parts is not called for and, what is more, seems to have little to add.

Turn now to Brahms's Third Symphony, and the culminating echoes of the symphony's opening motive that occur in the closing measures of the composition, some forty minutes later. It is hard to imagine a more effective and moving conclusion than that passage, in the wake of all that precedes it; furthermore, it is undeniable that the passage's virtues as experienced rest at least partially on the similarity between beginning and ending across a significant temporal span. Suppose, though, once again, that a listener were to carry explicit attention to this relationship as the final phrases are sounding. What would be the consequence? Is there, apart from a plausible cognitive pleasure in recognizing identities, a heightening of the impressiveness of these final phrases, an intensification of their sense of aural rightness or appropriateness in context for such a listener?

In such a case as this, I am inclined to think it just possible that intellectual awareness may fuse with aural apprehension, and so manage to afford a nonnegligible increment on the plane of basic musical comprehension. To bear the relationship in mind as the symphony concludes perhaps causes one to hear and feel more acutely, and not just to acknowledge, the ultimate fittingness of the symphony's coda.

Here is another example in this vein, one in which large-scale reflection operates in the forward or anticipatory rather than the backward or recollective direction. Beethoven's *Eroica* begins, famously, with two *forte* strokes for full orchestra, immediately followed by the Allegro's principal theme in E-flat, a straightforward, almost neutral proclamation by the cellos, tinged only slightly for the darker at its tenth note, a chromatic C sharp, which clashes with the G and B-flat sustained by the other strings.[15]

To one familiar with the *Eroica,* however, this opening statement cannot be heard to possess the same innocence a first-time auditor might invest it with. A third-time comprehending listener knows, in an implicit and dispositional manner, of the fearful extensions and manipulations the tune will be subject to during the development, and as a result the opening becomes for him more portentous than it first appears. He *hears* it differently than on first exposure, feeling its implications for the future more intensely and registering its character of concealed gravity more clearly than does a neophyte listener. Let this degree of difference be admitted. To what extent, though, does conscious anticipation of the development section to come contribute to this heightening or modification of the aural impressiveness of the *Eroica*'s initial utterance?

As in the example of Brahms's Third Symphony, it seems plausible that the major share of this effect is attributable to repeated listening and internal processing, without conscious reflection on the course of the movement as an architectural shape. Still, it is hard to avoid the suspicion that explicit forward awareness would translate itself into at least some increase on the level of aural involvement with the music.

What probably goes on in such cases as these, we may conclude, is this. A currently audited bit, figuring in a certain relationship to some other bit or bits, seems already apt or effective, in virtue of tacit processing of the relationship, and yet bringing the relationship to consciousness augments the sense of aural aptness or effectiveness to a small extent.

Yet even this admission may be overly generous. For surely it remains difficult to say whether in such cases we really have an augmentation of aural apprehension—that is, the experiencing of musical impressiveness more fully—rather than a purely contemplative apprehension, the pleasure of which is then superadded to that deriving from progressive grasp of impressive musical substance itself. I feel unable, in my own case, to pronounce conclusively on this point. So without discounting the notion

15. One is reminded of the basically cheerful and forthright quality of the melodic material here by Mozart's overture to *Bastien et Bastienne,* one of his early singspiels, which features a prefiguring of Beethoven's theme.

of such augmentation entirely, to view it as likely of an extreme subtlety would seem the path of discretion.

Finally, even if in the final analysis we recognize cases in which there is some augmentation of the aural effectiveness of a given bit owing to explicit awareness of large-scale relationships in which it figures, we should not lose sight of a key Gurneyan observation, one invoked earlier, which considerably weakens such recognition as a concession to architectonicism. That observation concerns what the locus of attention is when awareness of large-scale relations has this augmenting effect. That locus, Gurney reminds us, remains squarely the present event, which gives up none of its predominance to events not aurally present. The part currently sounding persists as the center of regard, and not the distant part to which it is related or the relation that exists between the parts. The gravest concession, it seems, that can be wrung out of concatenationism in virtue of such cases is the acknowledgment that awareness of a bit's *relatedness* to this or that temporally remote portion of a piece might sometimes enrich aural experience of the bit, and not what would concede considerably more, that awareness of *relations* per se in which bits figure markedly enriches the experience of those bits.

After the close attention we have just accorded to challenge 1, it is unnecessary to review where we stand vis-à-vis challenge 2. For the question whether there are nonnegligible augmentation effects of explicit apprehensions of large-scale forms on moment-to-moment listening is just the worry we have been addressing above writ large, and we have at least provisionally made our peace with it. In any case, the result of our specific inquiries in this chapter was fairly plain. In the case of sonata form in particular, the outcome was that there did not appear to be significant augmentation of aural grasp of music in virtue of such apprehensions on the part of one who is already hearing-as-a-sonata in the perceptual or tacit sense, that is, one who has the right sort of backgrounded, moment-to-moment involvement in the music's evolution from start to finish.

So we can turn shortly to the issue directly raised by the third challenge to concatenationism, which concerns the effect of conscious awarenesses or reflection not so much on the perceived impressiveness of individual bits experienced in context—our main focus so far—but rather on the *sensed cogency of succession of bit on bit, or part on immediately preceding part.* The focus of challenge 3, in other words, is the issue of *transitions.* Now as we noted in our initial exposition of Gurney, even the rightness or impressiveness of individual bits—motives and phrases, for example—is for Gurney assimilable to the general idea of cogency of succession, where the successive elements here are not, as ordinarily, whole motives or phrases but just individual notes or intervals. Still, it is convenient to treat the two matters somewhat separately, especially as there does seem to be a qualitative difference between the two phenomena, as exemplified by the difference between the wholeness of a single motive of a measure or so and that of a complete melody or musical passage.

In any event, there may be, where transitions are concerned, grounds for recognizing a more substantial relevance of large-scale cognition for small-scale basic musical apprehension than we have witnessed so far. Let us then explore the matter in the next chapter.

# chapter seven

# FURTHER CHALLENGES I

. . . there are no bridges in good music . . . good music is always meaningful, between the tunes as well as within them.

—Hans Keller, *Criticism*

I turn now to the third of the challenges to concatenationism articulated earlier, that conscious awareness of or reflection on large-scale relationships can affect the perceived cogency of a given transition from bit to bit. A transition, in my sense, is a musical hinge of brief duration, typically lasting a few measures, at which there is a succession of one musically homogeneous bit on another, the bits so joined usually being distinct rhythmically, melodically, harmonically, or in all three ways. Now we could see the cogency of transitions as just a special case of the impressiveness of individual bits, by taking such transitions themselves to be bits, grasped as such at the moment they occur. A transition "bit", then, would be the only somewhat artificial stretch of music comprising the concluding portion of a first, homogeneous bit, $\alpha$, and the initial portion of a succeeding homogeneous bit, $\beta$. And indeed, for a piece of music that exhibits cogency of succession throughout, transition bits are likely to have some psychological reality; that is to say, quasi-hearing of the end of $\alpha$ and the beginning of $\beta$, centered on the transition moment itself, is likely to occur.

Because transition bits, so to speak, have a lesser psychological reality than more traditional and familiar musically homogeneous bits, and because the quality of cogency or impressiveness in a transition is a rather special one—for example, the impressiveness of a bit of the ordinary sort to a large extent comes across out of context, whereas the impressiveness of a transition largely does not—it is convenient to consider the issue of influences on perceived cogency of transition as somewhat separate from that of influences on the perception of the impressiveness of bits in general.

### *Cogencies of Transition*

The concatenationist position on the registering of transition cogencies would have to be roughly as follows. Given tacit and nonreflective absorption of a piece's progression to the point just prior to a particular transition, given retentive memory regarding the course of the piece's continuation derived from earlier auditions, and given active listening to the moment in question, generating around it a small span of quasi-hearing, in which perceptual as opposed to merely reflective grasp of any significant relationships within this span can occur, then whatever degree of cogency is present in the music will be adequately registered by the listener with no need for any conscious apprehensions of formal relationships in which those transitions figure. But is this in fact so? It seems the only thing we can do is examine the experience of following some transitions with understanding, to see whether large-scale awarenesses superimposed on the process just sketched affect comprehending listening for the better. To this end, I have chosen to look at Tchaikovsky's Fantasy-Overture *Romeo and Juliet,* a composition rich in, among other things, transitions (figure 8).

One of the salient dimensions of this music is the programmatic one: *Romeo and Juliet* is a tone poem, with a literary aspect and representational content that complete appreciation would clearly have to acknowledge. But I take the liberty here of ignoring that dimension entirely (save for the labels I allow myself in designating the overture's various themes and motives). Tchaikovsky's tone poem hardly lacks for the quality of construction that makes it work on the level of pure music, as the experi-

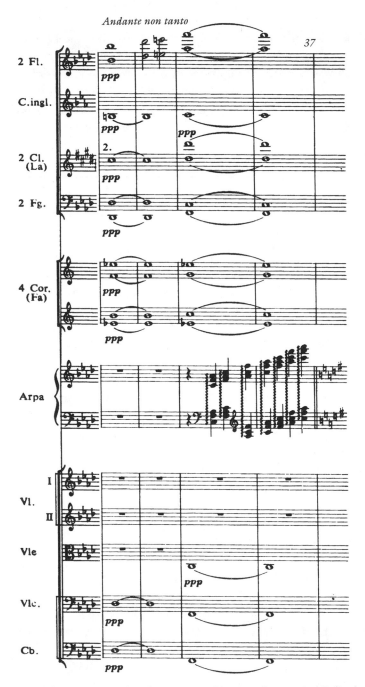

Figure 8. Tchaikovsky, Fantasy-Overture *Romeo and Juliet* (excerpts)

Figure 8. *Continued*

Figure 8. *Continued*

Figure 8. *Continued*

ence of many listeners who pay little or no attention to its programmatic side attests. In any case, I will treat it as such for the purposes at hand.

Here is a detailed breakdown of the piece, emphasizing its discernible joins, with measure numbers given in parentheses:

(*a*) Andante moderato, f-sharp minor: "fateful" theme (clarinets, bassoons) (1–11).

(*b*) Slow chromatic counterpoint (12–20).

(*c*) Key change to f minor, "rolling thirds" in cellos, ascending variant of "fateful" theme in winds, capped by harp glissandos (21–37).

(*d*) Effect of acceleration through reduced note values, pizzicato, in strings, "fateful" theme in winds, marcato (38–51).

(*e*) Reprise of slow counterpoint, "rolling thirds," "fateful" theme in strings, harp glissandos (52–77).

(*f*) Key change to a minor, timpani sounding a sustained E, falling figures in strings as horn scale rises chromatically, marcato (78–89).

(*g*) Allegro, full orchestra, on motive derived from "fateful" theme (90–96).

(*h*) Slow counterpoint, leading stringendo to alternating chords between strings and winds (97–111).

(*i*) Allegro giusto, b minor, full orchestra statement of "marital" theme, with prominent trochaic ("machine-gun") rhythm (112–121).

(*j*) "Whistling" figures, derived from "machine-gun" rhythm, traded between winds and strings (122–125).

(*k*) Fugato on "martial" theme, begun in cellos and basses, involving various modulations, accumulation of "whistling" figures (126–142).

(*l*) "Frenetic" section, scurrying strings with misplaced forte rhythmic accents from timpani and winds (143–150).

(*m*) Reprise of "martial" material (151–160).

(*n*) Scurrying strings, winding down to "whistling" figures, effect of deceleration through longer note values, leaving horns and cellos to effect modulation (161–183) to

(*o*) D-flat major "love" theme, on English horn and muted violas (184–191).

(*p*) "Rocking thirds" in strings, ending with upward rushing chromatic scales in flutes and oboes (192–212).

(*q*) Restatement of "love" theme for flutes and oboes, with "sighing" figures in horns; theme an octave higher than before and given its full extension, of thirty measures (213–242).

(*r*) "Rocking thirds" in harp, while winds sluggishly trade fragments reminiscent of "love" theme, becoming almost static (243–272).

(*s*) Development section: key changes to a minor, return of various themes, in combination: "fateful," "martial," Allegro motive, "scurrying" and "whistling" figures (273–334).

(*t*) Climax of fortissimo trombones and "machine-gun" motive carried by remainder of orchestra, in alternation (335–344).

(*u*) Reprise of "frenetic" section (345–352).

(*v*) Reprise of Allegro material, and firm return to b minor (353–364).

(*w*) Plunging scale in strings, followed by "rocking thirds" in winds over "scurrying" figures traded between first and second violins, ending in rushing upward triplets in strings (365–388).

(*x*) Third appearance of "love" theme, now in D major, on full strings with piccolo, with sustained triplet chords in winds (389–418).

(*y*) Fragments of "love" theme, interspersed with rushing string figures (419–440).

(*z*) Brief reprise of Allegro material, with some further working out, eventually slowing down and thinning in texture (441–484).

(*aa*) Closing: key changes to B major, B pedal tattoo on timpani, reminiscences of "love," "rocking," "fate" themes, return of harp glissandos, brief allusion to Allegro ("martial") material in last four bars (485–522).

This division into sections or semi-independent, fairly homogeneous units might, of course, have been carried out somewhat differently. My carving of the roast is similar to and only slightly more fine-grained than the carving represented by the assignment of rehearsal letters in my study score: 27 versus 22 units, respectively.[1] Even my carving would have had to be rather more fine-grained if I had been concerned to make every such unit strictly quasi-hearable, or apprehendable as an almost-present sonic whole. As it is, some of them are, while others, probably being spannable only by two or three acts or phases of quasi-hearing, are not.

1. Editio Musica Budapest, 1986.

Grouping these units into larger chunks, we may note at the outset that the piece can be seen as falling loosely into sonata form.[2] Under such a construal sections, *a* through *h* constitute a rather extended introduction, including three changes of key; sections *i* through *r* constitute the exposition, with three principal themes ("martial," "love," "rocking"); sections s and *t* are the development; section *u* is bridge to the recapitulation, consisting of sections *v* through *x,* and sections *y* through *aa,* finally, serve as a rather extended coda.

. . .

Let us now consider some of the points of transition between the sections or units identified in my outline. I will take it as noncontentious that Tchaikovsky's *Romeo and Juliet* is an aesthetically successful composition, well formed, expressively rich, and musically absorbing. In particular, I will take it that its joins are, in virtually every case, effective, that the movement from part to part is generally, in Gurney's sense, highly cogent. This is not to say that every succession is the antecedently most probable, or that every succession maximizes continuity, but only to say that each is compelling and convincing—that each "sounds right"—to an attuned listener familiar with the music. It is hard to see how the piece could be improved by subtraction, addition, or replacement of any of its components, to invoke Aristotle's famous dictum on organic unity in the *Poetics.*

Begin with the transition from *c* to *d,* which represents the first quickening of pace in the overture. As the pianissimo chords and harp glissandi fade away, the pizzicato string march commences, with the "fate" theme on winds above (see figure 8). It might be thought that this transition will be more effective—seem more apt, more cogent—if it is accompanied by conscious recollection of the opening presentation of this theme, thirty measures earlier—a distance clearly too great for quasi-hearing synthesis to bridge. But experience does not, I think, bear out this contention. The transition is felt as perfectly satisfying without any such explicit reflection.

There seem to be two simple reasons for this effect. (1) Even though the initial presentation in f-sharp minor is too far back to be quasi-heard with its subsequent marcato presentation in f minor, it is so recent that it is still vibrating, as it were, in aural memory, without the benefit of

2. As noted, for example, by Gerald Abraham in *A Hundred Years of Music,* p. 207.

a direct summons. (2) The rising pattern of four chords (with harp accompaniment) that concludes section *c* has a strong gestalt resemblance to the "fate" theme, and since that conclusion can be quasi-heard with the onset of the marcato statement of the theme at the beginning of *d*, the progression from *c* to *d* feels highly organic to an attuned listener, even when large-scale reflections are absent. The conclusion of section *c* in effect warms up the ears for the reprise of *a* that occurs in *d*.

The transition from *h* to *i* has a rather different character. Here stringendo b minor chords alternate between strings and winds, accelerating through the division of whole notes into half notes, until abruptly, at measure 112, the full orchestra, in rhythmic unison, erupts in the new, strident ("martial") material of the Allegro giusto (see figure 8). Now this transition, by contrast with the preceding one, is startling, arresting; it brings one up short, and arguably is intended to do so. Obviously enough, not all cogent transitions—for so I count this one—are of the smooth, seamless, evolutionary sort. What large-scale reflections might conceivably be relevant to this transition? And would any such enhance its perceived cogency? The only thing that seems to be a candidate here is explicit cognizance of the loose sonata structure mentioned earlier, and so awareness, say, of measures 105–111 as the end of the introduction per se and the beginning of the exposition proper, in the composition's main key (b minor). But while this awareness might afford a certain satisfaction as one grasps the (perhaps not very complex) construction of this composition, it is hard to see how it could make the specific transition appear more cogent. More plausibly, grasp of its particular cogency depends on close attention to the way the b minor triad emerges out of the slow counterpoint of measures 97–104, with the violin sliding prominently from A-sharp to B, the alternation and quickening of the chord thus arrived at in measures 105–111, and the subsequent assimilable, if unexpectedly assertive, proclamation of measures 112–115. And these are nothing but small-scale, quasi-hearable connections and correlations. The cogency of this transition, it seems, is not to be found outside it, in intellectual awareness of its position in a global structure.

Consider a third instance. The famous 'love' theme, in its first complete appearance (measures 213–242), is preceded by the "rocking third" motive eventuating in a rising chromatic scale in sixteenths for flute and oboe (section *p*). Its second (and last) complete appearance (measures

389–418) is preceded, again, by the "rocking third" motive with additional activity in the violins, and eventuating this time in pyramiding, rising chromatic scales in triplets for the strings (section *w*). There is thus a rough parallel, though with interesting small differences (key, rhythm, orchestration) between the earlier and later usherings in of the piece's most celebrated melody.

We can now ask our familiar question: Does explicitly holding in mind this rough parallel, at the point of the later transition, enhance its working or efficacy? It is difficult to see in what way. The correlating might provide a certain cognitive satisfaction—a balance sheet of musical features in two columns—but it seems unnecessary for these transitions, with their subtle differences from each other, to come off well at their respective locations. The attuned listener senses that the later ushering in is similar but not identical to the earlier, and this sensing enters into his finding the later one cogent in just the way it is, but forming the reflection explicitly adds nothing on that score.

We have so far failed to find any transitions in *Romeo and Juliet* whose aural cogency unmistakably depends on or is even plausibly aided by awareness of formal relations. I suggest that there may be none. And though as regards this question we obviously cannot undertake to accord to other extended compositions the same close attention we have accorded to *Romeo and Juliet,* there seems little reason to think that what goes for *Romeo and Juliet* would not go, by and large, for any piece of tonal music of the sort we are interested in.

But let us assume, for the sake of argument, that there are some clear cases—some specific junctures in some specific pieces—where awareness of some aspect of large-scale form affects, for what seems the better, the sensed cogency of part-on-part or moment-to-moment progression. It still does not even follow that one thus *should* engage in such reflection at these points. One would have to argue, independently and generally, that listening synoptically—that is, with attention to large-scale relations and overall form—is always the correct way to listen to a musical composition. And I doubt that one can do so.

Which is the true cogency of a particular transition, one might ask— that which it appears to have when overall structure is simultaneously contemplated, or that which it appears to have when listening is, so far as conscious awareness is concerned, wholly present-focused? Ways of listening that make pieces seem better or tighter are not thereby necessarily correct, nor are they necessarily ways of listening that reveal a piece's true nature. Perhaps if synoptic contemplation or awareness invariably made passages, and transitions in particular, more effective and satisfying, then apparent cogency under such conditions could be allowed to be the true one. But our review of *Romeo and Juliet* makes this supposition implausible. It is even likely that, given a certain sort of large-scale relationship, attending reflectively to that relationship may in fact diminish the sensed cogency of a particular transition, since attending to features of musical architecture often, if not always, entails some loss of attention to the small-scale features of currently passing musical fabric.

My conclusion from this discussion and the preceding musical review is twofold. First, whatever potentiation of perceived cogency of transition by large-scale awareness may occur is, in all probability, quite minor. Second, in those cases, if any, where it does occur, it is not necessarily proof of the appreciative correctness of sustaining such awareness, or always constitutive of an advance in basic understanding.

The fact is that cogencies of transition, when present, are assured by a piece's being appropriately constructed, such cogencies being conveyed to a listener through his tacit and nonreflective registering of that construction, in all its aspects. Cogency of this sort does not importantly rely on awareness of the place of any transition in the musical scheme as a whole, or on its relatedness to anything else at far remove. What is affirmed, once again, is that the large-scale structuring of a piece, involving relationships beyond the span of quasi-hearing, despite substantial causal relevance to the musical experience of a listener, has a claim on appreciative attention that is tenuous at best.

### Facilitation of Basic Understanding

The upshot of our consideration of the first three challenges to concatenationism is that architectonic awareness—reflective contemplation of large-scale relationships or overall forms of a largely spatial sort—has not been shown to be essential to the achievement of basic musical understanding, nor has such awareness been shown to play any significant role in enhancing either the perceived impressiveness of individual parts or the perceived cogency of individual transitions from part to part, once basic musical understanding of a given piece has been achieved.

But can architectonic awareness, granted it is not necessary for the attainment of basic musical understanding—repeated, stylistically informed listening sufficing for that—perhaps *aid* in the attainment of basic musical understanding, the capacity to quasi-hear a composition progressively from beginning to end, to the extent that it allows? Here the answer may very well be yes.

It is important to see that this question is strictly distinct from ones we have so far wrestled with. A form of the question addressed in the preceding section, for instance, is this: If aural cogency has been achieved in a listener's experience of a given composition, does large-scale reflection enhance or augment such cogency for the listener? Our reply has been largely negative. But a form of our present question is rather: If aural cogency has not yet been achieved in a listener's experience of a given composition, might large-scale formal reflection, engaged in prior to or concurrently with listening, facilitate or accelerate its achievement? A negative answer to the other question does not foreclose an affirmative answer to this one. It is indeed plausible that large-scale reflections, deliberately invoked or sustained, might enable one to listen in a certain way, focus in a particular manner, so that whatever cogency is present in the musical progression, though elusive up to that point, would be allowed to emerge for the listener on the basic, moment-by-moment level. What is strictly unnecessary for a given aural result could nevertheless be contingently friendly to its occurrence.

. . .

The issue of whether engaging in large-scale reflections might hasten one's aural grasp of a piece's fundamental progression has an affinity with the issue of whether score reading, either before or during audition, can aid one's musical comprehension of an extended composition. The issues are related, but they are not identical. One reason they are not, clearly, is that a listener might intellectually apprehend the overall form and large-scale relationships inherent in a piece without benefit of a score, the question of the effects of such apprehensions on listening experience being then as posable as ever. A second and more important reason is that not all of the conscious insights obtainable from a score are concerned with large-scale relations or overall form. Some of them are concerned with small-scale relations and properties, and consist essentially in the perceived application of descriptive labels or analytic categories to phenomena well within the compass of present-focused hearing and the quasi-hearing to which it gives rise.

Let me illustrate. By studying the score of *Romeo and Juliet,* one can learn such things as that the sequence of principal keys traversed is f♯, f, a, b, D♭, b, D, b, B; that the introduction, broadly speaking (measures 1–89) is roughly twice as long as the coda, broadly speaking (measures 481–522); that the passages that usher in the "love" theme at its two appearances (at measures 213 and 388) are similar but subtly different; that the texture of the orchestral writing—that is, the number, complexity, and independence of instrumental lines—generally increases throughout the introductory section, and so on. These would count as aspects of large-scale form, and their being entertained in thought would exemplify large-scale apprehension.

But one might also, and equally well, learn from a perusal of the score such things as that the opening dirgelike statement of the first measure consists of diatonic triads voiced on doubled clarinets and bassoons; that the third phrase of this statement has a contour resemblance to the second phrase without replicating it exactly; that the passage (measures 11–20) that follows the opening dirge begins on a note (C♯) shared with the concluding chord that precedes it; that this passage is imitative in its first six bars, involving repetition of a rising half-step figure. These surely count as small-scale connections and features, ones whose presence might be signaled, in an articulate way, by the score. They are also ones, I claim, whose presence can be registered and character felt in acts of present-focused listening, in contrast to the sorts of features and connections noted a moment ago, which are arguably apprehended only through reflective contemplation.

The question before us, then, is not that of whether score reading in general can facilitate basic musical understanding, but whether large-scale awarenesses—whether derived from score reading or not—may plausibly do so.[3] I will thus put to one side the issue of whether technical

3. Here is one writer confident of a positive answer to the question: "concentration is definitely assisted by study of the score—not during, but after a performance, and just before the next" (Philip Barford, *Bruckner Symphonies,* p. 49).

descriptions or analytic conceptualizations of small-scale musical features, which are typical fruits of consulting a score, can facilitate the aural grasp of such features as they contribute to musical cogency. On that matter I will just assume two points. I will assume first that such conceptualization or description is not necessary for these features to be heard and grasped or for their contribution to musical progression to be felt and registered.[4] (One need not know, for example, that there are clarinets and bassoons in the opening statement of *Romeo and Juliet* in order to register their specific combined timbre and sense a partial identity to the combination of clarinets and flutes that soon follows. And one need not conceptualize measures 11–16 as imitative in order to hear and actively connect in quasi-hearing the succession of overlapping half-step figures that conspire to give this passage a singular and disquieting tonal darkness.) Second, I will assume that in cases where they have not yet made their full effect in a listener's experience of a passage's musical substance, conceptualization or description of such features may contribute to their doing so. That is, such description or conceptualization might serve to focus listening attention on aspects of a passage's progression or fabric that had, until then, for whatever reason, escaped aural assimilation. (For example, keeping in mind that a certain passage contains a canon at a distance of one measure between highest and lowest voices can help one to hear it as such, or, more important, to hear or register aurally more of the musical fabric from moment to moment than one had previously done.)[5]

So, our topic clarified, are there then convincing cases of large-scale reflection that facilitate the achievement of basic musical understanding? I believe so.

---

4. Compare Budd, "Understanding Music": "In general neither the lack of a certain concept of a particular phenomenon nor the inability to recognize instances of the phenomenon as falling under the concept prevents a person from being sensitive to the presence of the phenomenon in a work of art and alive to the aesthetic or artistic function of the phenomenon in the work. . . . To experience music with musical understanding a listener must perceive various kinds of musical processes, structures, and relationships. But to perceive phrasing, cadences, and harmonic progressions, for example, does not require the listener to conceptualize them in musical terms" (pp. 246–247).

5. I would instance here, from my own experience, the Menuetto of Mozart's Wind Serenade in c minor, K. 388. Peter Kivy, in *Music Alone,* invokes to similar effect the opening tutti of Bach's Sixth Brandenburg Concerto, with its ingenious canon in the upper voices at a distance of half a beat, though he then goes on, characteristically, to overemphasize the role that intellectual grasp of the movement's canonic structure plays in comprehension of the music (pp. 116–117).

The last movement of Antonín Dvořák's Seventh Symphony, in d minor, opens with an unusual theme characterized by an initial octave leap and a semitone descent onto an accented beat, followed by a winding motion that finally comes to a rest a fourth below the tune's opening pitch (see figure 9). This opening serves to launch a complex, relentless exploration, in which that initial theme and others subsequently introduced are put through strenuous and inventive paces. In almost all of its appearances after its initial one, the opening tune is shorn of its introductory octave-leaping half-notes. At the very end of the movement, however, some thirteen minutes later, there occurs a Maestoso D major passage for full orchestra that opens with a gesture (measures 425–426) reminiscent of the way the principal theme is introduced at the outset, octave leap and all (see figure 9).

Now, this Maestoso passage serves as a very effective peroration for this grand concluding movement, and its power is invariably felt after several hearings of the symphony. Still, on first hearing it may seem to come too much out of the blue on the heels of a driving, marcato passage with little melodic substance and in the prevailing minor mode. Here is a case where explicitly keeping in mind the long-range connection—the degree to which measures 425–426 echo measures 1–2—might very well facilitate one's eventual aural acceptance of that Maestoso declaration as inexorable and fitting, when and where it occurs. Put otherwise, while the attuned listener eschewing long-range awarenesses might reach the stage of finding the ending appropriately convincing—unexpected yet ultimately satisfying—after perhaps four or five hearings, the attuned listener allowing herself such awarenesses might get there in three.

As another illustration we can look to the Chaconne from Bach's Partita in d minor for solo violin. A monument of implied counterpoint and emotional probing, Bach's Chaconne is, no doubt, a compelling musical discourse from its opening statement to the reprise of that statement some thirty variants later. However, the cogency of the joins from statement to statement, it is plausible to suggest, might be absorbed and accepted more readily if chaconne structure, and the regular repetition of a basic harmonic progression or ground bass that this involves, is before the mind as such. The consciousness that each successive eight-bar statement is, on some level, a variant of the preceding one may help one to hear them issuing from one another with the proper sense of rightness at each juncture, particularly those at which there is relatively

Figure 9. Dvořák, Symphony No. 7 in d minor, 4th movement (excerpts)

Figure 9. *Continued*

more surface dissimilarity or discontinuity, (as, for example, between the seventh and eighth, or the fifteenth and sixteenth). It is also quite possible that reflective consciousness of the movement as forming a chaconne might bring one more quickly to the point at which the significance of the whole musical journey is heard and felt in the final statement that brings the movement to a close.

We need not multiply examples any further. The lesson is already plain. One can find cases, perhaps with some difficulty, where large-scale reflection might plausibly be thought to foster attainment of basic musical understanding, or the aural synthesis at its core; call this effect *aural facilitation*.

Three things, however, should be emphasized in this connection. One, such facilitation is not so obvious that it might not, in a more skeptical light, vanish almost completely. Two, such facilitation as is robust testifies only to an instrumental, as opposed to intrinsic, value of attention to large-scale form. Three, and most important, such facilitation is just that, and not an absolute prerequisite or sine qua non of aural synthesis; nothing we have acknowledged here implies a condition the listener can achieve only by engaging in large-scale reflection. Occasional and modest facilitation of aural synthesis by large-scale awareness is something concatenationism can well live with. That such aural synthesis itself is basically concatenational in nature still stands firm.

I venture another summing up of the issue at this point. Intellectual awareness of structural relations may sometimes be helpful in getting one to hear something in music, but the latter is itself a nonintellectual matter, a matter of perceiving-as. Intellectual awareness of large-scale form, then, does not on this score contribute directly to musical understanding, but only indirectly, through fostering a kind of perception or aural grasp. What finally should be stressed, however, is that even such contributions are closer to being the exception than the rule. Most often, I suggest, intellectual apprehension of large-scale form has no noticeable influence on the rate at which music gels for a listener on the plane of basic musical understanding.

.　.　.

By way of concluding this chapter I address, with the hope of putting to rest, another possible problem for the concatenationist perspective, one of a different order from those included on the official schedule of challenges drawn up in Chapter 4. Someone might claim that reflective or contemplative grasp of large-scale form is really *continuous* with the synthetic quasi-hearing of small-scale progression, rather than completely different from it in nature; that is to say, that there are not really two distinct kinds of process or experience involved, but only one.

Thus Meyer argues, in *Explaining Music,* that all units in a musical work are processive at some hierarchic level; that is, that we feel them as moving toward goals, hear them as forming wholes with other events, ones that bring them to closure of some sort. This claim is meant to apply to passages, sections, movements, and even entire pieces. Does this mean, then, that there is no distinct quasi-hearing span? That any series of units can be quasi-heard if it is hierarchially ordered toward a closure of the whole? That an entire symphony, if sufficiently powerfully organized in its tonal implications, can be almost-presently-heard with its closing notes? Can the notion of quasi-hearing be expanded indefinitely, so that the distinction between it and the supposedly contrasting intellectual contemplation dissolves?

I think not. Quasi-hearing is a phenomenon, if I am right, marked by a certain phenomenological quality, and not one stretchable indefinitely, whatever the degree of hierarchic ordering of the music involved. Take the opening of the rondo of Schumann's Piano Concerto, discussed earlier. The rondo's initial phrase has the flavor it does because it evokes for a listener, consciously or not, the first movement's theme, but the listener simply does not quasi-hear the rondo opening with the first movement across the gap of the Intermezzo. Or recall our review of a listener's involvement in Mozart's Sonata K. 311, which suggested that quasi-hearing did not extend even to the whole of the first section in the tonic.

Perhaps, though, it would be reasonable to admit that some of the theoretical continuum between quasi-hearing and intellectual apprehensions of spatialized form is indeed occupied. We might want to recognize apprehensions of connectedness between widely separated musical units that, while not amounting to quasi-hearing—of which the constitution of melody out of a mere succession of notes is paradigmatic—are yet not purely intellectual, but somehow also perceptual as well. That there may be gray areas between the sort of aural synthesis of small stretches of music I have denominated quasi-hearing, which results in a sense of events almost heard together, and the purely contemplative apprehension of far-flung units represented in diagrammatic manner, does not dissolve the real difference between them or undercut the central role of the former in constituting basic understanding of music of any type. There is no more reason to think such intermediate, semiperceptual relatings of widely separated architectonic elements, if and when they occur, are any more necessary to such understanding than the most purely abstract apprehensions of large-scale structure.

It might also be charged, in a similar spirit, that what counts as directly perceived by a listener—as aurally grasped rather than merely intellectually apprehended—changes as one undertakes analytic study of music. I do not mean to deny this charge, but it does not tell against my main thesis, which is not that what is perceptually accessible in music is absolutely fixed, but rather that basic musical understanding, whose core is a certain sort of experiential grasp of and response to music, is both the largest part of the appreciation of music and something attainable without analytic study of musical form, merely through repeated, appropriately backgrounded listening. It may very well be true that the span of aural awareness for a given kind of musical discourse varies from person to person and with increased training or practice, but I am inclined to wager that for most people the maximal such span is not very great. In any case, with respect to the vast majority of music, basic musical understanding is attainable by listeners whose span of quasi-hearability remains decidedly modest.

There is perhaps insufficient reason to affirm, with Gurney, the absolute impossibility of aural grasp of large-scale structure. What is to be stressed, though, is that the normal listener capable of attaining basic musical understanding for a given piece of music quite demonstrably lacks any such aural grasp. And there are reasons, after all, to which we have appealed, rooted in the sequential nature of music, the limitations of present consciousness, and the nature of active remembering, for thinking that awareness of that sort cannot be of very broad span in anyone. Broad-span aural apprehension may not be impossible, but it is inherently difficult, contraindicated by the temporally unfolding nature of music, and unnecessary, in any case, for basic appreciation of music. Certainly the aural facilities of the very gifted, such as Mozart—if the accounts of his mental powers be accepted at full strength—cannot be determinative of what fundamentally makes music valuable for the majority of normal, practiced music lovers. If music is to be good it must be aurally synthesizable, ideally throughout its course, by those of moderate, rather than exceptional, quasi-hearing abilities.

# chapter eight

# FURTHER CHALLENGES II

Encountering a new piece of music is not unlike making a new acquaintance. In both instances, increased familiarity will bring greater understanding.

—Anthony Storr, *Music and the Mind*

You will recall my suggestion, in Chapter 5, that the largest part of a musical work's aesthetic content—most important, its expressive dimension—resided in its individual parts and their succession; in other words, that the foundation of musical expressiveness, the expressiveness of individual passages, was something clearly accessible to present-focused, quasi-hearing-based listening. Arguably, however, this is not all there is to the expressiveness of extended compositions, or all there is to the other aesthetic features that such a composition might display. It certainly seems, at first glance, that there are expressive and other aesthetic properties of musical works that are not comfortably locatable in individual parts, and so perhaps not appreciable just through nonreflective attention to the present. The question to be faced is thus roughly this: How much of a piece's aesthetic or expressive character is conveyed by the quality of its parts, heard in context, and how much only by contemplatable large-scale relationships among such parts?

## Higher-Order Aesthetic Properties

Before looking to examples to help us answer this question, we should recall that not all aesthetic properties that might be thought to exceed the resources of a concatenationist view of music listening—properties commonly thought to involve a global basis, and therefore to demand a synoptic approach on the part of a listener—are properties that in fact do so. One such property, discussed earlier, is that of unity, in the sense of phenomenal or hearable unity. As our discussion in Chapter 5 indicated, this property can in the main be quite plausibly construed in terms of a capacity of music to sustain an experience of local coherence, of part fittingly following and organically connecting with preceding part. The appreciation of most instances of what is called unity in music, then, may call for nothing more than involved perceptual absorption in the sounding substance of a composition. For the property of unity, in such cases, can be analyzed as effectively inhering in the composition's parts, in that if the parts individually fulfill certain conditions, that is, generate certain impressions or support certain experiences, then the composition as a whole can be said, in virtue of that, to exhibit the property.

This approach holds promise for accounting, by concatenationist lights, for other aesthetic properties of music akin to unity in seeming to require a broader awareness of musical expanses than concatenationism allows. Take, for example, grandeur, and consider its manifestation in something like the elaborate contrapuntal finale of Mozart's *Jupiter* Symphony. Is the grandeur, the gloriousness, that we register necessarily the upshot of sweeping reflections taking in the progression of the movement as a whole or large sections thereof? I would say not. The successive parts themselves can, as it were, directly convey the gloriousness of the whole. Because each added bit is, potentially, richer than the one that precedes it, it is in a position to partially reflect and incorporate those predecessors. The grandeur of the movement can be related to and grounded in a growing impression of richness, as part succeeds part, earlier bits progressively enriching later bits, which accordingly seem to burst with accrued musical interest when they finally reach the ear.[1]

---

1. There is an analogy here with what some philosophers have had to say about the structure of human memory itself. Henri Bergson, in works such as *Time and Free Will* (1899) and *Matter and Memory* (1905), compared a person's memory to a snowball rolling down a hillside, ever increasing and yet retaining within itself as it expands its earlier stages. More recently Richard Wollheim, in *The Thread of Life*, has emphasized how at least certain central types of memory encode past experiences in a very real sense, in that the emotional force of those experiences is preserved within and transmitted to the memory itself, though in weakened form.

Figure 10. Mozart, Symphony No. 41 (*Jupiter*), 4th movement (excerpt)

Consider a passage fairly far along, in the coda of this unusual sonata movement.[2] The passage I have in mind occurs sixteen measures after the second double bar, and comprises the last series of full statements of the movement's principal four-note motive, beginning with forte horns and bassoons and eventuating in the most profusely packed episode of the movement, wherein all five significant thematic ideas previously exposed are miraculously combined (figure 10). This culminating passage is glorious in virtue of how it sounds and what it conveys, occurring when and where it does, as the successor of all related earlier passages. The Olympian quality of that final series of restatements is in part a result of their seeming, at that juncture, likely to be the last such restatements, and the truly Jovian power epitomized in the contrapuntal complexity that ensues obviously relies on prior presentation of its component strands in less densely textured contexts. Much the same can be said of the very

2. For an account of some of the movement's singular features and what they require for full understanding, see Stephen Davies, *Musical Meaning and Expression*, chap. 8.

Figure 10. *Continued*

Figure 10. *Continued*

concluding passage of this finale, beginning sixteen measures from the end, announced by a familiar dotted figure—a sort of annunciation—with its snaky descending tail, repeated thrice and giving way to a conventional but welcome blaze of tonic assertion in full orchestra. In a good performance, this passage has the overwhelming effect in context that it does because of all that has preceded and built up to it, registered by the attentive ear, without any explicit harking back to passages that likely underwrite this splendid payoff (for example, the earlier similar descents near the outset of the movement).

In a piece as masterfully constructed as this finale, the potential for increasing richness as the structure progresses is realized to a very high degree, and in a way the events toward the latter half of the piece reap the harvest carefully sowed in the earlier half. The structure is built up bit by bit, and can, as far as grasping its grandeur is concerned, be adequately experienced bit by bit. This is because the structure has been arranged to make the successive parts—each heard as it occurs without

benefit of reflective retrospection—progressively more full and meaningful. Just as the sense of a movement's being unified can be accounted
for in terms of how individual parts are heard and grasped, so the total
impression of a movement's grandeur might be accounted for in terms
of more local qualities such as richness or resonance being felt to increase,
generally, from earlier parts to later ones. Conscious apprehension of the
whole that is grand, or of the whole that is unified, may be unnecessary—
unnecessary for either the experience or the judgment of that grandeur
or unity.

I offer one more illustration in this vein. In the course of the broadly
fugal finale of Beethoven's Piano Sonata in A-flat, opus 110, the attentive
listener experiences an almost continuous buildup and increase in tension,
which, however, achieves a remarkably total release and completion in
its final, carefully prepared measures (figure 11). Is the appreciation involved here plausibly just of the individual parts in succession, as opposed
to the whole per se? Is the aesthetic quality or effect just noted—buildup
and release of a broad-span sort—accessible to listening that forgoes
synoptic apprehension for nonreflective immersion in the developing
moment? It seems possible to give a positive answer, if one keeps firmly
in view that experiencing each bit of music is experiencing an element
in a sequence in which later members are enriched and illuminated by
those that precede them, and that experiencing the final gesture (measures
209–213) in particular is experiencing it not in isolation but rather as
the intended destination and culmination of all the musical gestures that
lead to that point, and at the same time as the satisfying echo of an
arpeggiated passage, perhaps not consciously recalled, near the beginning
of the sonata's opening movement (measures 12–13). Hearing and absorbing successive events as they occur is sufficient for the experience of
mounting tension in the midst of the finale, and having heard and absorbed all the foregoing proceedings, in all movements, is sufficient for
experiencing that singular unifying release that the last four measures are
so brilliantly calculated to provide. Thus the only sort of "appreciation
of the whole" clearly implicated by grasp of the qualities in question
appears to be, again, just memory-funded experience of successive parts,
woven together in stylistically appropriate informed acts of quasi-hearing.
Of course, there may also be superadded to this experience certain pleasures of a purely intellectual nature—which we will shortly examine in

Figure 11. Beethoven, Piano Sonata No. 31, op. 110 (excerpts)

Figure 11. *Continued*

their own right—but the fundamental musical reaction just described seems well within the grasp of strictly concatenationist listening.[3]

. . .

Convincing as this treatment may be for certain high-level aesthetic properties in certain musical contexts, it is doubtful that it can prove adequate for all such properties and contexts. For a number of important aesthetic effects in music do not seem susceptible of analysis as the cumulative sum of effects registered at and referred exclusively to

3. Another example can be briefly noted. In auditing the middle section of the second movement of Dvorak's A major Piano Quintet, an attentive listener receives a delicious impression of something endlessly cycling, winding back on itself, yet seeming always new. Does this impression require conscious grasp of or reflection on the total pattern of repetition? I claim it does not.

individual parts. Such effects are thus not such as can emerge for a listener who entirely eschews all forms of large-scale awareness going beyond the present and its quasi-hearable penumbra. Let us consider some
examples.[4]

We can begin with perhaps the most familiar item in the standard
repertoire, Beethoven's Fifth Symphony. The triumphant character of
the finale, from the forthright triadic proclamation of its opening theme to
its extended, perhaps overextended, conclusion—blazing and hammering
away as if C major were the only key in the world—is noted by every
listener and by the most casual critic. Doubtless the movement by itself
merits the appellation "triumphant," and would come across that way
if heard in isolation. But the specific quality and density of triumph
involved are arguably dependent on context.

Now part of this context is supplied, to be sure, by the passage immediately preceding the finale proper—a passage some of Beethoven's con-
temporaries doubted was music at all—in which we have the feeling of
being held in suspension, harmonically and rhythmically, and are filled
with uncertainty and expectation. This passage certainly colors the sort
of triumph we experience with the emergence of the finale's opening
theme (measure 374), and makes it in effect a kind of triumph *over*
obscurity or indefiniteness. But since the transition from tonal obscurity
to tonal definiteness in the course of fifty measures (324–373) is a continuous process within a relatively short span, it falls, I think, within the
compass of quasi-hearing, though at its outer bounds. In other words,
this passage might just be aurally graspable in such manner that the
specific coloring of triumph in which the passage eventuates can properly be registered without explicit backward reflection on a listener's
part.

The specific quality of triumph in the finale is also affected, however,
by the larger context of the symphony as a whole, and in particular by

---

4. It might be noted that all the cases to follow have one thing in common: they involve
compositions whose proper aesthetic understanding involves *retrospective* revision of or
addition to first impressions, thus implicating, to some degree or other, synoptic apprehension. But similar examples could have been offered, I believe, where the focus would have
been on aesthetic properties that depend on *anticipatory,* or forward-looking, reflections
for their discernment.

the finale's contrast with the scherzo, alternately mysterious and menac-
ing, and the opening movement, with its fateful and forceful pessimism—
both of which are, at the beginning of the finale, well out of earshot and
no longer aurally connectable to the musical argument then engaging
the listener. One might, in line with the approach to unity and grandeur
taken earlier, seek to hold that the specific triumphal quality of the finale
is conveyed to the listener in virtue of her having attended to and absorbed
the first movement and scherzo regardless of whether she explicitly recalls
those earlier installments of Beethoven's symphony. But in the present
instance this does not strike me as a very convincing maneuver. The sense
of the finale as a triumphant answer or rebuke to the pessimism of the
opening and the menace of the scherzo seems too conceptually laden,
too tied up with discursive thought to manifest itself to a listener without
explicit reflection on the course of the symphony as a whole and the
relations among its major divisions. The sense such a reflective listener
has of the symphony's dramatic import, it seems, cannot find an equivalent
in any sense that a strictly nonreflective listener, however attentively
absorbed in the music, can have of the symphony through aural synthesis
of the music on a part-by-part basis.

Further examples, involving other aesthetic properties, serve to rein-
force this conclusion. Francis Poulenc's Organ Concerto in g minor
opens with some very threatening gestures, rhythmically brusque and
grindingly dissonant, and continues in a dark vein for most of its course.
The world invoked musically in this concerto seems tragic indeed. Yet
soon come touches that temper this initial impression. The Allegro, with
its galloping string gestures and solidly minor tonality, is still rather
unsettling three minutes or so into the piece, but at that point there
develops, in contrast to the opening, an undercurrent of playfulness as
well. A thorough revisiting of one's first impressions, however, is called
for about three-quarters of the way through the work, when some unexpectedly gay, carnival-like music ensues. Soon after, with a brief allusion
to the opening gesture, the concerto concludes.

In context, the lightheartedness arrived at toward the end appears as
a polite thumbing of the nose at the earlier proceedings, and in particular
at the mood of doom and gloom that prevails throughout much of the
composition. The listener's estimate of the character of the opening

music, then, is subtly revised in retrospect; she regards its tragedy in hindsight as being tragedy only *entre guillemets,* as it were.[5] Once one has heard the entire piece, one is inclined to view it, as a whole, as almost a satire of solemnity. In gently chiding the gravity of the opening music, the nose-thumbing passage, and a few others to a lesser extent, serve to recast the quality of that opening as being more akin to mock-seriousness than real seriousness. There is here something of the tiger that turns out to be a pussycat: the organ's opening snarl doesn't seem as terrifying after one is aware of the calliope-like purring to come.

I think it is clear that these satirical dimensions of the Poulenc piece could not plausibly be perceived except through conscious reflection on the way individual sections of the movement at some remove from one another are related expressively.[6] Humor and wit, we may observe more generally, are the sort of aesthetic effects that necessarily presuppose comparative thinking at some level, and that may very well require an intellectual relating of items not in perceptual proximity.

It has been claimed, convincingly, that the first movement of Schubert's Piano Sonata in A, opus posthumous, presents a clear example of the expression of nostalgia in music.[7] We hear this in a brief coda to the movement, which comes after a rather long and leisurely essay in sonata form (figure 12). The coda consists mainly of a reprise of the movement's stately and highly rhetorical opening six-bar sentence, but with some important differences.[8] It is raised up an octave, played piano instead of forte, combined with tags from another theme, and then repeated in a

5. On first hearing, the equivocal nature of the opening naturally cannot be grasped until the arrival of what follows, and then only, it seems, through some act of conscious reflection. But on subsequent hearings, to progressively greater extent, this equivocal character will be apprehended right away, as the opening sounds, in virtue of the retention of what is to follow and consequent reflection on it.

6. The Organ Concerto contrasts, then, with other Poulenc compositions, such as the Concerto for Two Pianos, which alternate and intertwine serious and lighthearted materials right from the beginning, thus evidencing the music's basic aesthetic character from the outset, and obviating appeal to retrospective contemplation as requisite for taking hold of that character aright.

7. Charles Rosen presented a case for this interpretation in the course of a 1982 lecture-recital series in which he covered all three posthumous sonatas of Schubert; I am unable to say, however, if that case has ever appeared in print.

8. I say "mainly" because the coda is rounded out at the very end by arpeggios in A major and B flat major, an alternation that subtly evokes the rising semitone motion important throughout the movement.

Figure 12. Schubert, Piano Sonata in A, op. post., 1st movement (excerpt)

lower register. The mood is much gentler, and occurring when and where it does, the passage conveys a strong impression of wistful meditation on an earlier phase of a journey or a life. As one writer justly observes, "The effect of the whole passage in its context is extraordinarily moving."[9]

Now a concatentationist might well propose that the effect in context is secured by the construction alone, followed closely in a present-focused

9. Philip Radcliffe, *Schubert Piano Sonatas*, p. 46.

manner. But the question is, once again, how much of this context must be grasped, and in what manner, for the effect to emerge? I think it is clear the coda will have an effect, and a moving one, on any attentive and familiarized listener; it will resonate with earlier events, and acquire a flavor consequent on them. But for such a listener to hear the coda as specifically *nostalgic*—as arguably it truly is—might require her to reflect consciously on its gentle reminiscence of the opening statement and mentally recall the subsequent trials that that and other themes undergo in the course of the movement. The thought of something like a voyage or progress, over which the coda casts something like a backward glance, would seem to be required for the nostalgia in question to be explicitly recognized and fully experienced. Nostalgia seems too cognitively specific a state to be equated with, or approximated by, the effect of later passages on even ideal but nonreflecting listeners who have heard and followed all earlier ones in turn. With conceptually involved states such as nostal-gia—or triumph, or wit—music will typically embody them structurally, where it does so at all, in such a way that conscious reflection on large-scale structuring, and not just attentive auditing of moment-to-moment structure, will be required to discern or confirm their presence.[10]

My last two examples involve aesthetic effects that are, if anything, even more difficult to characterize than those in the three preceding examples. Richard Strauss's mellow oboe concerto, from his last years, is one of his finest works, and its sprightly finale certainly contributes to its excellence. But engaging as it would be heard entirely on its own, it is satisfying in a particular way, I believe, possessing a special welcomeness, when it is heard not only in its proper place in the concerto but against the conscious backdrop of the decidely more elegaic first movement. Heard in that fashion, the good humor of the movement carries with it an antidotal air of cheerful consolation in relation to the autumnal cast of its predecessor. Just having heard and retained the first movement, I think, does not suffice for the aesthetic effect I have in mind. If the

10. Perhaps another way to put the point would be this: Certain ways of realizing conceptu-ally complex expressive properties (e.g., triumph, humor, nostalgia, despair, hope, consola-tion) in music depend on structural embodiment or paralleling of those conceptual elements. The feature that ties all these psychological conditions together—roughly, their necessarily involving a contrast or comparison between different states, periods, or frameworks—is a feature that readily finds musical analogs.

impression almost of shaking off regrets is to manifest itself firmly, conscious awareness of the relationship of expressed sentiments between opening and closing appears to be called for.

If there are individual, wagerably unique forms of beauty, then surely the Adagietto of Mahler's Fifth Symphony must be the possessor of one of them. An important aspect of this beauty, though, arguably becomes apparent only when one reflects on the whole movement. It concerns its overall shape, and the way this shape evolves, from an expressive point of view. The best I can do to convey the impression the Adagietto as a whole affords is to resort to an image: that of a far-off land that gradually approaches from out of a mist, assumes a greater reality, and then recedes once again, soon seeming to have been perhaps only a dream or a mirage. The careful management of dynamics, instrumentation, intensity, melodic shape, harmonic suspension, and so on from point to point is of course the basis of the impression afforded, but the impression as such would seem to presuppose an image something like the one just offered, which in turn implicates something like contemplative review of the unfolding of the movement as a whole. The specific archlike shape of this movement, construed in the way proposed, helps undergird the powerful air of longing for something precious but lost that seems a fair characterization of the movement on an emotional plane.[11]

. . .

How can the concatenationist respond to all these observations? Clearly, to deny the appreciative facts I have taken some pains to detail, which strongly suggest that awareness of large-scale form has some role

---

11. Constantly shifting moods, juxtaposed segments of quite different character, and the superimposition of disparate frames of reference are commonly experienced with many of Mahler's larger movements. Conscious awareness of these elements contributes to the philosophical, world-embracing quality that is often registered in a Mahler symphony.

In the finale of the Seventh Symphony, for example, the rondo theme's appearances are separated by contrasting episodes, involving opera-parodic music, some of it reminiscent of Mozart's *Abduction from the Seraglio*. This rondo is admittedly significantly underappreciated by one who never engages in any reflection on its overall course. Where parody, quotation, or allusion in music play a significant role, broad-span reflective comparisons will obviously be required for their appreciation. But that sort of appreciation is rightly marked off from the basic musical understanding we have been at pains to foreground. One can have basic understanding of a piece of music without grasping its allusiveness, parodic aspect, or philosophical resonances—though of course with some music, of which Mahler's is a prime example, that would be to miss a fairly substantial, though still not the chief, part of what makes the music distinctive and valuable.

to play in the grasping of aesthetic content, would be of little avail. Instead, the concatenationist should simply endeavor to put these facts in proper perspective. This perspective is provided, I think, by the following reminders and observations.

It remains true, first, that the *largest* part of a piece's expressiveness is contained in its individual passages, and second, that *most* of that expressiveness is embodied in such a way that relations to distant passages, even when they contribute causally to such expressiveness, need not be brought to mind or attended to explicitly by the listener. The examples of high-order expressiveness recently reviewed may have given a misleading impression of the frequency with which expression in music calls for reflective apprehension. If so, let the difficulty I now avow I had in coming up with those examples stand as a corrective.

To clarify the issues further it helps to introduce some terminology. Let *isolated* expressiveness in music refer to the expressiveness of individual passages taken in isolation; let *contextual* expressiveness refer to the expressiveness of individual passages in context; and let *complex* expressiveness refer to expressiveness attributable only to sequences or ensembles of passages taken together. The distinction between contextual and complex expressiveness, note, is one regarding the possessor or locus of expressiveness, not the grounds or basis of such expressiveness. *Simple* expressiveness, that attributable to individual passages, may then be either isolated or contextual expressiveness.

If we look closely at the cases considered above—Beethoven, Poulenc, Schubert, Strauss, Mahler—we will discover that, with the possible exception of the Mahler, they are all cases of contextual expressiveness with complex sources, rather than cases of complex expressiveness as such. The triumphal quality of the beginning of the Fifth Symphony's finale, the nostalgia of the A major sonata's coda, the mock-terror of the Organ Concerto's opening, the spunky pluck of the opening of the Oboe Concerto's third movement are properties of those very passages, however relationally grounded. On the other hand, the quality of regretful longing in the Mahler—and perhaps the overall wittiness of the Poulenc—is possibly only reasonably ascribed to those pieces as a whole.

So the first point to make, at this juncture, is that significant *complex* expression, as I have defined it—which almost invariably requires large-scale awareness for its apprehension—is a rarer and certainly more elusive affair than the phenomenon of complicated *contextual* expression, which characterizes most of what is brought to light in our recent examples.[12] But a second point is that many cases of complicated contextual expression, or other contextually based aesthetic effect, are plausibly such as to come across effectively to part-by-part listening; that is, listening without explicit large-scale reflection. This was the case, recall, with the grandeur of the finale of Mozart's *Jupiter* Symphony, and might well be the case with features such as power, spirituality, tension, gravity, and haunting-ness. That is to say, a good deal of contextual aesthetic content in music is arguably a matter of later passages being primed or potentiated by earlier ones in such fashion that effects are experienced without apprehension of the relevant relations on an intellectual level. There are indeed, as we have lately allowed, cases of contextual expression that call unavoidably for reflective assessment, but it would be a mistake to think that all, or even most, contextual expression does so. For contextual expression, once again, is not as such the same as complex expression.

Next, it bears emphasizing that what there is of true complex expression in music—that is, expression that belongs properly not to any individual passage but only to a sequence of passages—is yet entirely dependent on and arises from the simple expressions possessed by such passages as sequenced. In other words, there is no such thing in music as monolithic, free-floating expressiveness, pervading the whole of a composition but unconnected to its parts. A piece is gay here, somber there, approaches calm at its midpoint, moves toward frenzy at its climax, stops short of bathos at its conclusion, and so on. To a substantial extent, if not entirely, the expressiveness of an extended piece of music just is the union of the expressivenesses of its parts, large and small, where the expressiveness of individual later parts, as we have seen, can be rich indeed. In any event, that dimension of a piece's expressiveness that goes beyond the expressive-ness resident in its parts remains wholly grounded in and emergent on those parts and their individual expressivenesses.

It is worth observing, finally, that it is not entirely clear that the very aesthetic properties involved in these examples most troubling to the

---

12. For a persuasive case of complex expression on a broad scale, involving the emotion of hope, see Gregory Karl and Jenefer Robinson, "Shostakovitch's Tenth Symphony and the Musical Expression of Cognitively Complex Emotions."

concatenationist—nostalgia, wit, consolation, longing, regret—are such as to be absolutely incapable of expression except through large-span relations among passages explicitly contemplated. Might not some musical passages express some of those properties—properties that in the cases we have been concerned with have rested on intellectually apprehendable relations between widely separated parts—but without doing so in that fashion? I believe the answer is yes. Of course I do not deny that the examples examined were and are indeed problematic for concatenationism. I suggest only that what is typically conveyed in music through architectonic devices might very well sometimes be conveyed through alternate means, ones transparent to present-focused listening.[13]

## Intellectual Satisfactions

We come now to what is perhaps the most obvious challenge to a concatenationist perspective, the fact that music, in virtue of its large-scale structuring, provides many opportunities for intellectual aesthetic satisfaction in structure, when such structure is recognized explicitly and made the object of contemplation. Apart from the roles it may be thought to have in amplifying congencies of transition, in facilitating aural synthesis, in giving access to aesthetic content, large-scale reflection on musical structure can very plausibly be maintained to be its own reward, in that it appears, in many cases, to afford its own sort of aesthetic pleasure, distinct from that of following moment-to-moment progression or of savoring emerging expressiveness. As before, my procedure will be to look at representative examples of this phenomenon and then consider

13. To attempt to elaborate this suggestion would take us too far afield, but what I have in mind, in essence, is this. Despite the conceptual complexity of these emotional properties, it is not logically impossible—as some philosophers, beginning with Hanslick, have argued—but rather coherently maintainable that single passages of music might succeed in expressing some of them, and furthermore, possibly without presupposing relations to passages at a distance. To be sure, these properties are perhaps most often conveyed through the offices of some kind of isomorphism in which the conceptual core of the emotion with its essential comparison of one state with another is one term, and a set of expressively connected musical passages is the other, but I believe there is no sound argument that they must necessarily be conveyed that way if they are to be conveyed at all. (For further discussion, see my "Hope in *The Hebrides*.")

what attitude toward them it seems appropriate for the concatenationist to adopt.

I must first distinguish the phenomenon I am concerned with from another that it only partially overlaps; namely, the possibility of deriving musical enjoyment from study of the score of a piece, either before or during the act of listening. As I observed in Chapter 7 with regard to the facilitation of the aural grasp of music, what can be gleaned from a score is, as often as not, insight into small-scale structure and the technical basis of local effects, as opposed to insight into large-scale form and the foundation of global effects, where these exist. A score of Mozart's Symphony No. 40, for example, might confirm that the main section of the Minuet movement owes its jerky swagger largely to a syncopation that Mozart achieved by tying the melody's third note across the bar line. Similarly, one might learn from a score of Beethoven's Symphony No. 1 that its somewhat disorienting opening gesture is a final-sounding V-I cadence, contrary to norms for the introduction to an eighteenth-century symphony. These sorts of cognitions—roughly, ones in which we appreciate the technical grounds for various perceptual effects that have already registered in audition—indeed provide a certain pleasure, albeit of a subsidiary sort, but clearly they do not involve reflection on large-scale relationships.

One might also mention a subtly different intellectual pleasure, founded in curiosity, just in discovering how a given musical device with which one is aurally and conceptually familiar is in fact notated; and a related yet somewhat different pleasure of learning, from perusal of a score, what the constitutive features of a familiar passage are as notation-ally determined, where this is not evident from hearing adequate performances, even if fairly coincident with one another.

On the other hand, it is clear that grasp of aspects of the large-scale architecture of a composition, whether or not abetted by score study, can in some cases provide pleasure of a similar sort. Surely this is orthodoxy in the music critic fraternity. One quotation will suffice: "Apart from the aural experience, there can surely be no reasonable doubt that part, at least, of our appreciation of a great work of musical art is grounded in our intellectual understanding of the constructional processes involved."[14] So it is to cases of this stripe, properly speaking, that we now turn.

14. Philip Barford, *Bruckner Symphonies,* p. 49.

. . .

We can start with a work of perhaps the first great composer in the Western tradition, Guillaume Machaut. Machaut, whose output represents the culmination of medieval music, penned many compositions notable for their ingenuity of construction, but possibly none more so than the rondeau "Ma fin est mon commencement." This roughly five-minute-long piece is in effect a musical palindrome, whose second half consists precisely of the first half played backward. I think it fair to say that even a highly experienced listener would fail to detect this merely upon listening. Furthermore, I submit that consciously acknowledging the palindromic technique while listening makes no difference in the listening experience itself.[15] Still, the palindrome structure can be corroborated by inspection of the score, and it constitutes a rather remarkable achievement, so we may finally allow that there is a certain aesthetic pleasure in reflecting on this structure while following the specific twists and turns of the musical fabric Machaut has so skillfully woven. Let this composition stand, then, as our purest example of music that affords a sort of intellectual pleasure in large-scale structure, a contemplation of pattern for its own sake, free of any complicating interactions with the aural synthesis of music as heard.[16]

Bach's Fifth French Suite in G affords a somewhat similar example, though one in which intellectual apprehension is, I believe, not so hermetically sealed off from the realm of the hearable. The Gigue of this suite, in standard binary form and compound triple meter, has one striking constructional feature. The sprightly three-measure theme of the A section is transformed, by the simple device of inversion, into the slightly

15. That this is so, I suspect, reflects the fact that the process of musical apprehension is so powerfully forward-looking, so much a matter of grasping the specific way each bit pushes toward and eventuates in its successor. This inexorable future-directedness of the listening process simply overwhelms and obliterates the reverse-ordered, steps-retraced structure that we may be intellectually aware informs the piece's latter half.

16. An instance akin to the Machaut, but from the twentieth century, is the opening movement of Bartók's *Music for Strings, Percussion, and Celesta*. It is a slow fugue that moves from A through various keys to a climax on the rather remote E-flat, and then back again to A, in which the latter, harmonically backward-moving half of the fugue features mainly upside-down forms of the fugal theme. Its quasi-palindromic aspect in respect to tonality is thus eerily seconded by the inverting of its thematic material halfway through. Awareness of this pattern during or after audition, even if it has no aural import, does seem to provide a certain—though rather rarefied—delight.

more dour but equally energetic theme of the balancing B section, the ensuing contrapuntal treatments in each case being rather comparable. This economy of means makes for an especially unified and satisfying composition. It may even be that explicit reflection on this architectural fact strengthens the effect of unity—recognizing the inversion relation between A and B might have a subtle effect on how the latter is heard— but in any case this reflection is the source of some additional pleasure in apprehending the piece. Armed with this large-scale awareness, one receives an impression of the Gigue akin to that which might be offered by a diptych whose panels present the same landscape, but from differing vantage points, or under different skies.

Of roughly the same order, I take it, would be the satisfaction in noting the family resemblance between certain gruff bass figures in the *Jupiter* Symphony's finale (at measures 9–12, for example), and those more spotlit ones that constitute the Jovian thunderbolts of the symphony's opening measures. This large-scale thought linkage, while perhaps unnecessary to make those passages in the finale seem a fitting and coherent counterweight to those in the first movement, can add a measure of aesthetic delight to the finale as one hears it unfold.

My next example involves a case of mirroring between microcosm and macrocosm, and is due to Roger Sessions.[17] It concerns the Scherzo movement of Beethoven's last string quartet, opus 135, in F. The understated opening theme of this movement is a curious syncopated affair that gently rocks its way through the tones A-G-F-G-A-G-F, which motion is then repeated immediately in a higher register. Sessions notes that this motion in the small scale among the tones F, G, and A adumbrates the harmonic motion to come in the excited middle section, during which Beethoven runs a rising scale idea through the keys F, G, and A in succession, reaching a fairly manic climax in A, and then subsiding back into F for a reprise of the first section. As Sessions suggests, the felt cogency of the movement undoubtedly owes something, causally, to this structural parallelism. But that apart, it seems plausible there is a distinct aesthetic pleasure in grasping this internal coherence of small-scale and large-scale motions on a purely contemplative level, once aural synthesis

17. The example is discussed in Sessions's *Musical Experience of Composer, Performer, Listener,* pp. 49–51.

has been attained and is not in question. This example, like that of the Machaut rondeau, seems a clear case of a large-scale architectonic awareness providing an intellectual pleasure, while the maintaining of such awareness during listening is without aural impact as such.

. . .

One of the most impressive large-scale structures in all music is arguably that of the concluding movement of Brahms's Fourth Symphony. It is in the form of a passacaglia, involving an eight-note bass theme that regularly recurs every eight measures, though in progressively transmuted guises. The passacaglia as a whole consists of an initial statement of the theme, followed by thirty strict restatements or variations, and capped off by a closely related, organically evolved freer coda of about twenty measures. In this coda a rising trombone motive (measure 273), later taken up by woodwinds, sounds a particularly fateful and sinister note, leading directly to the piece's shattering conclusion—a conclusion which, in a fine performance, can seem like little less than the end of the world. But what is perhaps most amazing about this movement is that the passacaglia basis, with the unfailing repetition that it implies, does not appear to hamstring the usual fluid developmental processes of the romantic symphony, but instead somehow coexists with them. Brahms's passacaglia has as much variety, as much tension, as much contrast of different ideas as the best sonata-allegro movements. It even has a plausible sectioning reminiscent of, though not equivalent to, the sonata's familiar arch form: exposition, e minor, statements 1–12; interlude, modulating to E major, statements 13–16; recapitulation, return to e minor, statements 17–31, with a clear climax in 25–26, then a second, briefer interlude at 27–29, in G major, followed by final reaffirmation of e minor in 30–31; coda. In short, instead of something like the paradigmatic effect of passacaglia form—a sense of steady, cumulative accretion to a fixed musical substance, as in Bach's magnificent example of the genre for organ[18]—what is experienced is something more akin to normal dynamic symphonic process, though with a quite special and unmistakable quality of inexorability, a quality that it is not hard to believe is rooted in Brahms's unique fusion of an impassioned symphonic rhetoric with a relentlessly repeating, though constantly transformed, ground bass.

18. Passacaglia and Fugue in c minor, BWV 582.

Now, the power of this movement in audition—and it is perhaps the most powerful piece of music that I know—does not depend on a conscious grasp of the idea of a passacaglia (or chaconne) or on any comparative thoughts based on such grasp.[19] Yet there is, I suggest, a deep and aesthetically germane intellectual satisfaction to be had in reflectively contemplating Brahms's success in achieving the unlikely fusion just noted. One cannot help but marvel that such a fluid and organic musical embodiment of—let us say—the seriousness and tragedy of human existence in fact breaks down, coda apart, into thirty-one distinguishable units of strictly equal length, each involving the same small-scale harmonic motion.

. . .

In the middle of the nineteenth century, composers began to be quite drawn to a compositional idea known as "cyclic form," which involves the bringing back, in later movements of an extended piece, of themes or thematic materials deriving from and identified with earlier movements. Listeners were expected to recognize these visitations explicitly and associate them with their original contexts of occurrence. The main point of such cyclicity was the attainment of a species of higher-order unity for the piece as a whole, dependent on a listener's reflective grasp of the circular shape thus effected by such returns.

A famous example is the review of the principal themes of the preceding three movements at the beginning of the last movement of Beethoven's Ninth Symphony. More typical, though, and almost as well known are the recurrence of a motto theme in every movement of Tchaikovsky's Fifth Symphony, and the moving eruption in full orchestra of the plaintive slow movement theme of Franck's Symphony in the middle of its finale. In Béla Bartók's *Music for Strings, Percussion, and Celesta,* to take a more modern instance, the slow fugal theme of the opening movement is brought back to great effect in the midst of the frenzy of the concluding movement.

As more subtle manifestations of cyclicity, we may recall the liberating flourish with which Beethoven concludes the massive fugue at the end

19. Musicologists disagree on whether or when "passacaglia" and "chaconne" can be used interchangeably. A prevailing view is that a passacaglia involves a repeating ground bass, a chaconne a repeating chord sequence (thus implying a succession of root tones, i.e., a ground bass). The difference, if any, is irrelevant for present purposes.

of his Piano Sonata opus 110, which flourish is strongly reminiscent of the A-flat arpeggiation near the very beginning of the sonata, and which has not been heard in any form for fifteen minutes or so (see figure 11). A rather similar gesture, though without the same release-valve effect, is the echoing, in the concluding measures of Brahms's Third Symphony, of the falling fourths of the first movement's opening theme, in this case spanning a gap of close to half an hour (see figure 3). Perhaps subtlest of all is the allusion in Mendelssohn's *Hebrides* Overture to the opening fragment of the piece's big D major theme, an allusion mysteriously effected, in b minor, by solo flute in the piece's final bars.

In most cases of this type it does seem arguable that, in addition to the hearable or intuitively felt unity imparted to a composition by these sorts of repetitions, a distinctly intellectual satisfaction can be had through a reflective apprehension of the rounded shape achieved by thematic recycling over large spans, and a contemplative consideration of the sense of finality and homecoming implicit in its use.

．　．　．

In sum, what staunch anti-architectonicism seems to overlook is that large-scale, not strictly hearable or quasi-hearable formal patterns can be a source of direct satisfaction in music, of a more intellectual sort than that provided by close attention to the flow of musical substance. What is overlooked is that a proper part of the experience of a piece of music is wholly reflective, involving imaginative contemplation of its larger shapes, balances, structures, and overall course. In appreciating a symphonic movement, for example, and even more in seeking to comprehend the full canvas in which such a movement has its place, one clearly experiences a kind of pleasure in actively building up the structure in memory as the music advances, and consciously reviewing its emerging shape in imagination.[20]

So what should a good Gurneyan—or conscientious concatenationist—say to this array of intellectual satisfactions in large-scale form and large-scale structural relationships? A number of things, none of which

20. For a discussion of this activity, under the label of "co-construction," see Paul Hindemith, *A Composer's World*, chap. 2. Naturally I contend that Hindemith greatly overstates the importance of this activity, engaged in on a conscious level, to a listener's understanding of music—whatever the importance of activity analogous to that in the process of musical composition.

deny what these examples in common allege, but which place it instead in the right light.

To begin, recall an observation made in Chapter 5, that there is a difference, not entirely scholastic, between a piece of music itself—an aurally experiencable sequence of tones—and the structure or form of that piece of music, exhibited at some level of analysis. These are not identical, even if the temptation to identify them is greater than it is for, say, a human body and its form. First, a piece's form, in the analyst's sense, is more abstract and less particularized than the piece itself. Second, a piece's form, in the sense analysis provides, is essentially spatial and static, while the piece itself is inherently temporal and directional. Thus to grasp the one perceptually is not surprisingly distinct from, and not necessarily continuous with, grasping the other intellectually.

Even though its form or structure is clearly an aspect of a piece of music, so that grasping a piece is grasping something that has a certain form and has been structured in a certain manner, it is not therefore necessarily a grasping of that form or structure itself, and vice versa. So even if we acknowledge the sorts of intellectual satisfactions recently noted, there is at least some justification, based on a distinction of objects, for denying that such satisfactions are taken in the music—the piece of music per se. What the present-absorbed, attentive, and backgrounded listener understands and consequently enjoys—the music in its developing immediacy and full sonic particularity—is not quite the same entity as the totality of abstracted structural relationships and patterns that the intellectual appreciator beholds, wholly or in part, and in the grasp of which is afforded an enjoyment of a different kind.

But let us pass on to a more important rejoinder the concatenationist can make to the claims of intellectual pleasure in apprehension of large-scale form. Such pleasure is not only different in kind, not only directed on an object distinct from that on which basic musical understanding is focused, and not only clearly unnecessary for such basic understanding to occur. In addition, such pleasure is, first, manifestly *weaker* than the enjoyment consequent on basic musical understanding, and second, strongly *parasitic* on the achievement of basic musical understanding and the degree of enjoyment derived from it.

I take it as plain that the pleasure derived from reflectively contemplating a formal pattern or relationship exhibited in some piece of music one has experienced or is experiencing is simply not comparable to that attendant on following a complex web of music with perceptual understanding, connecting its parts together, one by one, in successive interpenetrating aural syntheses. The spontaneous, unforced, almost palpable relating, within a span of quasi-hearing, of proximate musical events into a flow virtually present at one time offers a satisfaction that all who truly love music must admit is vastly more vivid and intense than that which can be afforded by deliberate and concerted relating of widely separated musical events under the aegis of some form concept in an act of intellectual cognition. Required somehow to choose, one would never give up the latter for the former.

That brings us to the second point. The pleasure we take in intellectual apprehension of the large-scale form or structuring of a musical composition seems largely to presuppose the greater and more fundamental pleasure we take in its perceptually apprehendable sequential substance. That is to say, our interest and satisfaction in large-scale form are not so much interest and satisfaction in it in abstracted isolation as they are appreciation of such form in connection with music as known to us experientially. It is not, thus, palindromic shape or passacaglia patterning or cyclic recurrence per se that please us in the above examples, but those forms contemplated as grounds of the aural cogencies, aesthetic effects, and expressive results that we have already apprehended in the music we know as dynamic process.[21] Awareness of large-scale relations in music would have little appeal for us if it were not related to values already realized in a given composition on the plane of locally absorbed listening.

Consider a piece of music with unarresting themes, uninteresting harmonic development, incoherent instrumentation, transitions of minimal cogency, and in general progression of a sort that either totally stymies quasi-hearing or else bores it into submission—but suppose that this piece displayed some intellectually apprehendable patterning of the sort we have discussed. Who would care? Who would take the trouble to ferret it out and hold it in mind? Clearly, no one. For what relish we have in being aware of such patterns seems predicated on their being the operative patterning of something we have antecedent interest and delight in, on a more fundamental level.

---

21. For more on the conception of aesthetic pleasure underlying these remarks, see my "What Is Aesthetic Pleasure?"

Thus my intellectual pleasure in the large-scale form of the finale of Brahms's Fourth Symphony, say, is not detachable from my much greater and prior pleasure in it as a dynamic musical occurrence, aurally grasped, but is instead completely dependent on it. I marvel, in reflective awareness, at the wedding of the passacaglia pattern to the compelling musical discourse I know from experience, whereas the pattern itself, apart from that, is not anything to marvel at. A certain proportionality seems in operation here: the greater the satisfaction in a piece on the level of basic understanding, the greater the potential superadded satisfaction in intellectual reflection on aspects of large-scale form that appear to underlie, or at least coexist with, its basic success as music. Review of the nature and interrelations of the pleasures and understandings involved in other examples recently mustered (Machaut, Beethoven, Franck, Bartók) would, I suggest, only confirm this judgment. The intellectual apprehension of formal relationships, patterns, and devices is powerless to really engage us unless we have first grasped the music on the basic aural level. That grasp requires no consciousness of anything beyond the pale of quasi-hearing, and the satisfaction to be taken in such intellectual apprehension as also occurs tends to be, all things being equal, in rough proportion to the value of the music as grasped on the basic, that is, concatenationist, level.

We can perhaps now see the great mistake of those who advocate attention to large-scale form as the prime object of musical comprehension, before a piece has cohered in hearing in a listener's mind. It is that the rewards such attention can provide are effectively unavailable at that stage. Intellectual contemplation of aspects of large-scale form is aesthetically virtually meaningless to one who has not gotten the musical substance of a composition, part by part, into his or her "inner ear." One must have largely internalized the fundamental, dynamically progressive form of a piece of music before conscious contemplation of aspects of large-scale construction can have any experiential payoff, can contribute an additional sense to the music, can afford its own special measure of delight in the interaction between listener and musical entity. Even then, of course, it behooves us to remember that it is essentially icing—though sometimes of a most impressive sort—on the musical cake, and not the cake itself. The basic point is that if the cake is not in place, there's nowhere for the icing to go.

Our review of the major challenges to concatenationism is concluded. We have obviously made some accommodation to some of them, which was naturally to be expected. There would, after all, have been little point in confronting objections that could be swept away without a trace. But it is equally the case that concatenationism, as a view of what is fundamental in a listener's understanding of music, has come through largely intact. Call the result *qualified concatenationism*. Then qualified concatenationism, I think, has been vindicated, at least for the bulk of the music that makes up the Western tradition. In the final chapter I offer, from a qualified concatenationist perspective, some further reflections on the topics of value and form in music.

# chapter nine

# CONCATENATIONISM, MUSICAL VALUE, AND MUSICAL FORM

> There is no more to prevent you or I from turning out a string of bars
> in the form of a sonata than to prevent us from turning out a string of
> lines in the form of a sonnet or a tragedy in five acts and in blank verse.
> It is not the form that baulks us of a Shakespearean immortality, but
> the inordinate quantity of first-class stuffing that is required to make
> these forms, long, severe, and tedious as they are in themselves, interest-
> ing, or even endurable, to any but the performers or the author.
> —George Bernard Shaw, *London Music, 1888–89*

What Gurney held about the ground of musical value can be
simply stated, as can his rationale for holding it. The central value of a
piece of music is to be measured, surely, by the value of the experience
it affords suitably prepared listeners. Now the core experience of a piece
of music is a matter of how it seems at each point—how interesting,
cogent, right, expressive, and so on[1]—a matter of the character and
quality of each part as it comes. The core experience of a piece of music
is decidedly not of how it is as a whole, or even of how it is in large
portions, since one never has the whole, or large portions of the whole,

---

1. The problem still remains, however, what exactly that property is—whether denominated
cogency, rightness, or fittingness—that should ideally be instantiated by any segment of
music, including transitions between segments, if the piece which they as a whole constitute
is to contain as much musical value as possible. Aural cogency is manifestly not the same
as visual coherence, nor is it the same as logical consistency, yet neither is it being such
that no other continuation is thinkable. It is a matter for further thought how best to
characterize this desired feature of musical substance, or alternatively, whether a single
characterization is in fact possible.

except in abstract contemplation. Because experience of the parts in sequence is crucial, and because experience of the whole or large portions of it is not, the value of the total experience—and thus, ultimately, of the piece of music—is to a good approximation just the sum of the values of the individual experiences of parts. This would not be to deny that some of those individual experiences, for instance, of the ending of a symphony, may be particularly fraught with meaning in virtue of experience of related earlier parts, and so contribute more to that sum than others. But that admission is consistent with there being no important musical experiences that have as their objects musical wholes of significant temporal extent.

I contend that Gurney is basically correct that the fundamental grounds for a positive evaluation of a piece of music must be on the order of the appealingness of individual parts and the cogency of their succession, rather than features of overall form or structure. Satisfyingness of later parts may be based on connections between such parts and much earlier parts, but such connections, unlike the experiences that they may underwrite, do not themselves provide primary reasons for positive evaluation.

.   .   .

Suppose we consider the admittedly contentious question of the *real* form of a piece of music. There are, it seems, a number of possible construals of this question, depending on how the stressed adjective is understood. One construal would be this: What aspects of a piece's form are *responsible* for the beauty, expressiveness, unity, and other positive aesthetic qualities that it has, or that enable the piece to provide the worthwhile experiences it does? And the answer is: Conceivably any such aspect. Good form in this sense is thus whatever form is casually efficacious, whether on a small or large scale, for muscial virtue. Another construal would be this: What structural aspects must be directly *attended* to for understanding to occur, for the above qualities to be grasped or the above experiences to occur? The answer to which our investigations have inclined us is that, in very large measure, it suffices for attention to carry to the music's constitution at each moment and to its connectedness of part to part within quasi-hearable spans.

Consider a claim to the effect that *X* is good music because of its form. If *because* expresses a casual explanatory relation, then in principle any aspect of *X*'s form might qualify; whereas if *because* expresses a relation of justificatory reason, then perhaps none strictly do, but only the degree of moment-to-moment cogency or rightness that $X$, however formed, is able to sustain. Now if the correlation between certain formal features, whether large or small scale, and aesthetic or experiential effects is regular, well established, and widely recognized, then the formal features in question may come to be considered reasons by proxy, as it were, for evaluative claims. But if so, it will only be because those formal features are understood or assumed to invariably have those effects.

The judgment that a piece has good musical form, if that judgment is to connect with and presumptively support a judgment of musical worth, cannot rest directly on the presence of this or that large-scale formal relationship. It must rather rest directly on registration of moment-to-moment satisfyingness or cogency. Though certain sorts of global relatedness may, as it turns out, conduce to such satisfyingness and cogency, it is not conscious apprehension of those global relations that makes a piece satisfying or cogent if it is so. So the essential form of music, as far as appreciation and evaluation is concerned, does not lie there. Music's real form, as Gurney might put it, is continuational and successional, not spatial and architectonic.

Let us take it that to say a piece of music is good as music is roughly to say that, when properly heard, the piece affords an experience intrinsically well worth having, in relation to other pieces of music or to the capacity of music for gratification generally.[2] Then a primary reason for positive evaluation of a piece of music would be a feature of music connected as closely as possible with the experiential potential centrally constitutive of a piece's goodness; it would be one with direct force in justifying a judgment to the effect that such-and-such a piece of music was good. A primary evaluative reason, where music is concerned, is thus a feature of a piece that loosely entails that experience of it will be of a certain kind, where that kind is antecedently acknowledged to be intrinsically worthwhile.

Examples of primary reasons for positive musical evaluations would be such things as *expressing intense sadness,* since this loosely entails that a

---

2. This is, of course, only roughly true. For complications and qualifications, and an acknowledgment of various instrumental goods that music may properly afford, see my "Evaluating Music." Experiential goodness, even if the largest part of the worth of a piece of music *qua* music, fails to quite exhaust it. In any event, it is the experiential goodness of music that I am exclusively concerned with here.

normative listener's experience will be one of intense expressiveness, and *exhibiting musical cogency,* since this loosely entails that a normative listener's experience will be one of progression and continuity. Examples of nonprimary reasons, by contrast, would be such things as *possessing overall form α* or *displaying large-scale relationship β*, which entail, even loosely, nothing as to what the listener's experience will involve. They will entail such only if architectonic contemplation is smuggled into what normative listening requires, and then only very loosely indeed.

.  .  .

The importance of good large-scale form in music must principally lie in the fact that if a piece is well constructed, successive bits will seem inherently interesting and cogently connected to their predecessors, where and when they turn up, even if in some cases they will seem so partly in virtue of sensed relations to much earlier parts. For example, a motive or phrase used both as a beginning and an ending of a musical paragraph is likely to strike one as satisfying when heard at the end, without one's thinking of or connecting it explicitly to the beginning, because one will have heard it before and will thus register it first as familiar, and then as somehow fitting and consummatory, when and where it recurs. Care must be taken not to slide between the proposition that if a piece were not constructed in such-and-such a large-scale way it would not sound as satisfying as it does, moment to moment and part by part, to an attentive listener, and the proposition that the piece is satisfying to an attentive listener precisely because he consciously grasps, realizes, or reflects on aspects of its large-scale construction.

The truth is that citing of large-scale formal relationships in a musical work is largely irrelevant to *evaluation* of the work, as opposed to *explanation* of whatever effectiveness it achieves. For evaluation must be based directly on the experiential payoff of properly appreciating a work. Formal analysis can explain, ex post facto, such experiential results, but it cannot, in the absence of such results, justify a critical evaluation. One can point to many large-scale features of a musical composition that do not appear to have any clear effect on a listener's experience of it, and which do not, when explicitly apprehended, make the composition seem any more unified or cogent than it already does.

.  .  .

It is useful, in this connection, to contrast the case of music with that of abstract painting. Awareness of large-scale relations is almost always relevant to appreciating and evaluating works of art of that sort. That is because large-scale relations within abstract paintings can be apprehended perceptually through normal viewing. In addition, such relations, when attended to, generally contribute to perceived unity or expression in a pronounced way.

Now one might object that even the viewing of a painting has a temporal dimension, in that our eyes are constantly flitting over the surface of an object viewed—fixing and refixing, as psychological studies have shown, with an amazing rapidity—and thus that the contrast between apprehending a symphony and apprehending a painting has been overdrawn.[3] But the fact that rapid eye movements are involved, imperceptibly, in normal visual processing, that now one part, now another part of an object is brought into transitory focus, in no way dissolves the real contrast between visual and aural grasp of extended objects of the respective sort. With a painting of ordinary proportions, whatever the mechanisms that underlie normal seeing, there is still something approaching a view of the whole, a grasp of the interaction of all its parts at one time, that is available to a perceiver. One can, both literally and figuratively, step back from a painting and behold it in its entirety, notwithstanding the fact that the fixation of one's gaze continues to shift, within a small compass, from instant to instant. But with a symphony such beholding is simply impossible; the work is never "there" for perceiving all at once. Memory and imagination may provide surrogates, of course, for purposes of inner contemplation, but at that point we have left perception behind.

. . .

Consider a movement M1, displaying all sorts of "rational" relationships—symmetries, balances, repetitions over large spans—but little cogency of succession of part on part. Consider a movement M2, with cogency of succession at every point but no discoverable, contemplatable large-span relationships of a "rational" sort. Which is better music? Without question, M2. Cogency of succession is clearly more important to musical worth than demonstrable large-scale balances, symmetries, or repetitions. But consider now movement M3, which has the virtues of

3. For an objection of this sort, see McAdoo, "Hearing Musical Works in Their Entirety." McAdoo is discussing my earlier exposition of Gurney's ideas in the essay "Edmund Gurney and the Appreciation of Music," noted in the Preface to this volume.

both M1 and M2. It seems unclear, at the least, how much better M3 is musically than M2. What these comparisons show, I believe, is the primacy of a concatenationist rather than architectonicist criterion of musical value, and the at best indirect relevance of large-scale structural features to the evaluation of musical works. Large-scale form may be of any particular kind, but its being of one kind rather that another, its being elusive or even unclassifiable, has no automatic bearing on evaluation.

The finales of certain Bruckner symphonies, most notably the Fifth, are perhaps examples of pieces possessing obvious large-scale organization which do not seem either better or worse for that. Not only is the whole, in several of those finales, best left aside, so far as a listener's involvement is concerned, but the music's organization in the large does not seem to contribute much causally, one way or the other, to its cogency in the small. The deficiencies of those finales have at base to do with the latter: individual passages, or the joins between passages, are too often simply not convincing. The music fails to move forward in the way that it should, a way that Bruckner shows to be possible in his musical idiom in most of his other movements.

Why, we may ask, is the music of Vivaldi and Albinoni superior to that of, for instance, Tartini? By and large, these three composers feature similar harmonies, similar rhythms, and similar figuration, and all rely rather heavily on sequence.[4] Is it, then, that the music of Vivaldi and Albinoni is superior in its large-scale form or patterning? Is that what accounts for its superior listening quality? Not necessarily—or at least not directly. The difference is rather to be located, in the first instance, in the greater impressiveness and expressiveness of the parts in Vivaldi and Albinoni as compared with Tartini, and in arrangements of part on part that generate expectation, build tension, go somewhere—in short, are absorbing—as opposed to those of Tartini, which more often than

---

4. Of course it might be said that the music of Tartini, coming a generation after the other two, is in a somewhat different general style than theirs—to wit, moderately more homophonic, and with phrase structure a bit closer to rococo. But the relative poorness of his music, I suggest, cannot be laid up to the modest shift in style per se. To make the comparison chronologically more exact one might take as a third term, say, Bononcini in place of Tartini. But in fashioning workable examples of this sort, capable of engaging intuitions, one quickly runs up against the problem that, in general, musical inferiority and obscurity are significantly correlated.

not fall flat.[5] One is usually bored with Tartini's sequences well before they conclude, and when one does conclude, one hardly cares what comes next. If music is unsatisfying—music of the traditional sort with which I am concerned—there is always, I suggest, some deficiency at the level of small-scale, quasi-hearable form. That is Tartini's basic problem, whatever further deficiency may be laid at his door with regard to large-scale form in its capacity as causally contributory to perceived musical cogency.

·  ·  ·

A concatenationist perspective on music helps to explains why Schubert's Eighth Symphony and Bruckner's Ninth Symphony can be considered great works of music, ones of the first rank, despite their lack of one or two movements originally planned to complete them—that is, despite the composer's being unable in each case to realize his multimovement architectural plan. For their greatness consists in the quality of the present-focused experience their existing movements readily afford, independent of the pattern they present to abstract contemplation. Concatenationism can explain why the phonographic offerings of thirty years ago titled "Fifty Great Moments in Music" and the like, involving excerpts averaging three minutes in length, while not representing perhaps the ideal approach to the classical repertoire, yet provided something of significant, self-standing value, whereas a visual analog of such offerings, say "Ninety Greatest Square Inches of Abstract Painting," complete on one sturdy cardboard-backed poster, would be little more than a joke.[6]

Concatenationism is also well suited to explain the difficulty of certain modes of contemporary music, ones that fly squarely in the face of the fundamental criterion of part-to-part cogency or compellingness of continuation which is at the heart of value in music of a standard sort. In

5. This is not to say that *none* of Tartini's compositions hold one's interest, the "Devil's Trill" Sonata for violin and keyboard being an obvious exception. But its interest, we may note, owes much to its singular pictorial qualities and exaggerated gestural manner.
6. Aaron Ridley advances a related insight in his discussion of what Tovey called "bleeding chunks," short musical excerpts presented out of context, without their musical surrounds. Though Ridley is more worried about the musical intelligibility of such excerpts than I am, he recognizes that they retain a substantial measure of musical meaning even in their detached state: "For of course by limiting the context within which the understanding listener forms expectations, the significance of an excerpt is not exactly the same as it would have been were it heard in its original surroundings. But it certainly does not follow from this that I cannot understand it at all" (*Music, Value, and the Passions*, p. 71).

place of the model of music as a developing chain or evolving process, some music of the postwar period—which continues today—presupposes a model of music rather opposed to that one: music as happening, music as frieze, music as sonic environment, music as meditative aid, music as combinatorial exploration, music as entropic phenomenon, and so on. It is natural that such music meets resistance among listeners cognizant of and comfortable with even the full range of music in the standard repertoire, for which a concatenationist mode of listening, I have suggested, very largely suffices. Nontraditional contemporary music calls for approaches to listening and habits of listening that traditionally oriented listeners will not possess, and which they may be loath, rightly or wrongly, to try to develop, perhaps fearing interference with the approaches and habits that have stood them in good stead with so much other music.

· · ·

The philosopher C. I. Lewis was one of the first modern exponents of a thesis, now widely accepted, of holism in regard to the value of a life. The thesis is that such value is not just the sum of the values of the life parts taken in isolation. Not unexpectedly, Lewis used musical compositions throughout his discussion as an illustrative analogy.[7] Nevertheless, a musical composition and a life, though evidencing some similarity, are also importantly different, and thus even if the thesis holds for human lives it does not automatically carry over, mutatis mutandis, to, say, piano sonatas. One salient difference is that a sonata, unlike a life, is fixed in advance, and its whole extent experienced repeatedly.

In any event, the concatenationist claim is not, after all, that the value of a composition is the sum of the value of its parts taken in isolation, out of all relation to their musical surroundings, but rather that it consists, very largely if not entirely, in the sum of the value of the parts occurring in just the order that they do, in relation to other parts of the piece. In other words, the basic claim is the denial of a significant value in the whole, gained through explicit apprehension of that whole, *over and above* that represented by the sum of the values of the parts. Certainly I would agree with Lewis, following G. E. Moore, that given the possibility of "organic unities," there is no logical guarantee that the listening value

7. C. I. Lewis, *Analysis of Knowledge and Valuation.*

of a whole is equal to the sum of listening values of its parts.[8] But what I have argued is that, in the case of music, when it is the value of "thick" parts—that is, parts in their proper musical contexts—that is involved, there is, because of the fundamental cumulativeness of the experience of music, in fact usually very little remainder.

So to concur with Gurney that the primary value of a musical composition is in its successively apprehendable parts is not at all to say that their connecting together is of no importance. Neither is it to deny that later parts can, through funding by earlier parts, have a richness denied to those earlier parts. Still, it must be said that in some compositions there is in fact so little real implication between parts, and so little funding of later by earlier, that the value of the whole could be fairly approximated even by the sum of the listening values of its separable parts, with no regard even for their order of occurrence. Perhaps an example is Schumann's *Humoresque,* op. 20, which exhibits almost no interconnectedness among its twenty-five or so distinct sections: the piece is a sort of aural kaleidoscope, in which nothing much would be lost by wholesale rearrangements, within limits, of the order of the parts, or by the deletion of some parts, beyond the resulting subtraction of their own values as parts.

. . .

It is worth briefly comparing music and narrative art forms, in respect of the issues with which we have been grappling. What is the relevance of explicit grasp of the large-scale form of a novel, compared to the corresponding grasp of a symphonic movement? A much stronger case, it seems, can be made for the necessity of such grasp to basic understanding in the former case than in the latter. Plot structure, character development, dramatic irony, and moral import are obviously of great concern in appreciating a novel, but arguably none of these things is a locally assimilable feature of a novel. One cannot be said to understand a novel, on any level, if one has no conception of the manner in which successive parts conspire to form an overall structure, no inkling of the relations between incidents and characters across large spans of the narra-

8. See G. E. Moore, *Principia Ethica,* chap. 6. An organic unity, for Moore, is a complex state of affairs the value of which cannot be assumed to be the sum of the value of its constituent states of affairs.

tive, no sense of the implications of the tale told as a whole. So large-scale connections, where narrative works are concerned, are clearly of central appreciative relevance. Now music would appear to have a narrative aspect. Must not, then, the same be said of it?

I think not. For despite a certain suggestiveness to the comparison, nonrepresentational music is not so much an articulate *tale* as a temporal *process*. The degree of analogy between literature or film on the one hand and music on the other is easily overstated. If one absorbedly tracks the evolution of a piece of music, if one registers its expressiveness throughout, if one intuitively senses what is happening and is about to happen at every point, than one basically understands that piece of music—or so I have tried to show in this book. Not so for literature and film. Standard novels and movies are above all else stories, with beginnings, middles, and ends, with characters who continue and develop throughout, with lives governed by causes and reasons, actions and reactions, all of which call for explicit recollection and synoptic integration for their understanding.

Let us admit, however, that there is some appropriateness to viewing at least some nonrepresentational music as in a loose sense narrative; the case for such appropriateness could be and has been made for the music of such as Beethoven, Schumann, and Mahler.[9] Would this admission militate against concatenationism, even for such music? Not necessarily. For there are two ways to look at narrative. One is the kinetic-dynamic way ("What's coming next?"), while the other is the spatial-architectonic way ("What's the big picture?"). Where it is important to hear music narratively, with respect either to purely musical continuation or to its semantic interpretation, it is arguable that the kinetic-dynamic way will often suffice. In other words, it may be enough for such understanding as music demands that at each point one has an appropriate sense of event arising out of and leading to event, but without ever taking a synoptic view of what the series of events from beginning to end means

9. There has been a fair explosion of intriguing work on this aspect of musical meaning, which full understanding of music on a listener's part would need to encompass; see, for example, Anthony Newcomb, "Schumann and Late Eighteenth-Century Narrative Strategies" and "Narrative Archetypes and Mahler's Ninth Symphony"; Fred Maus, "Music as Drama"; Lawrence Kramer, *Music as Cultural Practice, 1800–1900;* and Mark Evan Bonds, *Wordless Rhetoric.*

as a totality, without ever consciously reflecting on the fate of individual musical entities or ideas. To respond to music in such a way might just qualify as adequate involvement in and grasp of muscial narrative, I suggest, whereas it manifestly would not so qualify in cases of literary or cinematic narrative. Narrative is clearly less central to the import of music, if music can be made out to have such a dimension, than it is to the import of literature and film. Accordingly, a less reflective or intellectual response may suffice for substantial understanding even of music that displays such narrativity.[10]

　　　·　·　·

So much for the differences between pieces of music and fully narrative works of art. That narratives of a robust sort require global apprehension for their core comprehension does not, we have seen, imply that the same is true for music. Yet there are other sorts of cultural product which, like music, cannot be perceived as wholes, in that one must take in and digest their parts sequentially, but which it would appear must be understood as wholes, rather than as just sequences of parts, if they are to be understood at all. I have in mind such things as philosophical arguments, mathematical proofs, whodunits, treatises, and so on. One may be tempted to argue that if what we have been saying about the nature of musical form and musical understanding is true, rooted in the basic sequentiality of musical processing, then it would apply also to items of the above sort, with the result that we need not grasp arguments, proofs, whodunits, treatises as a whole in order to understand them, that we need have no regard for their overall form in appreciating them. This would thus be a sort of *reductio ad absurdum* of concatenationism.

The threatened *reductio*, however, is hamstrung. This is because such artifacts—let me call them "rational structures"—differ from musical compositions in several important ways. Those differences account for the differing roles that local and global apprehensions play in their respective comprehensions.

---

10. Again, I do not mean to deny that there are rhetorical and dramatic aspects of instrumental music that a listener may need to bring to reflective awareness in order to have a full understanding of music or a complete grasp of its content, especially for music from the eighteenth century on. I would insist only that such insight in regard to music does not play anything like the same role it does in regard to novel or film—namely, that of being a sine qua non of basic comprehension for that form of art.

First, rational structures are essentially propositional in nature, which makes it easier to grasp in an intellectual manner the relations among their parts, many of which relations are of a logical or evidential sort, and to represent those relations efficiently. But musical substance is not propositional, and the relations obtaining between parts of a musical composition are neither logical nor evidential.

Second, rational structures are governed by global objectives or ends definitive of the sort of thing they are, ones that are usually signaled at the outset of proceedings, for example, the establishing of some philosophical claim, the demonstrating of some geometrical theorem, the solving of some murder mystery, or the expositing of some scientific theory. The sequence of parts or steps in such a rational structure is designed, first and foremost, to fulfill the defining objective, which makes it imperative that the objective and what sequentially contributes to its fulfillment be brought into relation by the subject consciously and explicitly if understanding is to occur.

Third, the parts of a successful musical composition, appreciated when and where they occur, are generally valuable for their own sakes, as we have repeatedly observed, but this is much less true for the parts of a successful rational structure. Such parts have mainly instrumental value, the principal thing being always how they advance the overarching goal: establishing the conclusion, completing the proof, presenting the theory, articulating or resolving the mystery. In contrast to a part, or quasi-hearable stretch, of a piece of music, one step of an argument or whodunit has little intrinsic value. The value resides mainly in how all the steps fit together and answer to the overarching purpose that rationalizes the whole structure.

For these reasons, not to review an argument or whodunit as a whole after going through it in sequence would be to skip something crucial. But not to do so after listening to a piece of music attentively and responsively, while it might be to deprive oneself of some higher pleasure or deeper insight, would not in the same way be to miss the essence of the thing in question. Failure to step back from a rational structure and grasp it as a whole after perceiving it sequentially is fatal; failure to do something comparable with a string quartet is much less so. A musical composition, unlike a rational structure, need not as such have an over-arching goal that rationalizes its stepwise progress and to which the steps of that progress must be referred for their proper understanding and assessment.

Thus, to bring us back to the point of our investigation, though musical compositions and rational structures have in common being temporally extended and sequentially perceived, the fact that synoptic apprehension is critical for understanding and appreciating rational structures does not show that it plays a similarly critical role in the understanding and appreciation of music. So no *reductio* of a concatenationist perspective on music is forthcoming from that quarter.

A piece of music, unlike a rational structure, is an irreducibly perceptual affair. What this means is that no conceptual condensation of its core content is really possible, and no analytic distillation of its concrete form is central to its appreciation.[11] There is no alternative to simply apprehending its parts in sequence in all their particularity. But there is also no inevitable call to do anything more than that.

. . .

I now turn briefly to the perspective of creators and recreators of music, something I have sidelined in order to focus on music from the perspective of listeners. Consider statements to the effect that some performer has a good grasp of overall structure, or that some composer is a master of large-scale organization. I suggest that in many cases, despite appearances to the contrary, claims of both sorts can be cashed out in terms of apprehensions of parts, in a perfectly concatenationst spirit. The basis of such claims may often be just facts such as that the composer constructs the piece, or the performer performs the piece, in such a way that the listener finds each part, occurring when and where it does, to be satisfying both in itself and in relation to its neighbors.

For a performer to shape a piece well in large-scale terms, we may propose, means for the performer to attend to and project its large-scale form in such fashion that (1) it is convincing on the moment-to-moment level at which aural synthesis takes place, and (2) it affords intellectual pleasure in contemplation of that form, if such is to be had, during or after audition. There can be little debate that, in judging the success of

---

11. My point here fits with conclusions in an excellent study of musical experience, Mark DeBellis's *Music and Conceptualization,* conclusions to the effect that central aspects of basic musical knowledge are strongly nonconceptual and nonpropositional.

a performer's performative interpretation of piece, the first objective is of greater weight and importance than the second. Thus the primary meaning of a performer's shaping a piece well in the large scale is that it come off well, for listeners, in the small scale.

What shaping a movement well in large-scale terms cannot reasonably mean is shaping it so that its hearing as a whole, by attentive and experienced listeners, is maximally satisfying. As we have had occasion to observed, there is nothing in the audition of music that really deserves to be called "hearing wholes"—where the wholes in question are fairly extensive stretches of music, such as the movements of symphonies. One does not really *hear* such wholes as wholes; at best one hears individual parts and their immediate penumbras while projecting, in imagination, the past and future course of the larger musical argument. Of course a listener may be able to entertain, at various times, a spatialized conception of the full span of such a movement, but this has surprisingly little to do with the piece as music, as a developing process in and for essentially sequential hearing.

Since concatenationism is fundamentally a view about the understanding of music by listeners, in denying that spatial images of global form are necessary for such understanding it is not meant to deny that such images are of value to conductors and performers in their attempts to arrive at optimal ways to perform or structure pieces for legitimately present-focused listeners. A spatial grasp of large-scale form may quite plausibly enable a conductor, say, to make the right decisions about how a piece should be played, or shaped at each moment, so that its concatenational substance, as it were—which any successful piece of music must possess—is conveyed to a listener most effectively.[12]

The acceptance of concatenationism does not entail that a composition's large-scale form, and in particular that aspect of it sometimes referred to as "the long line," can be of no valid concern to conductors or performers, those charged with making music live for listeners. For it is doubtless true that attention to such on the part of a pianist, say, may produce a performance whose specific soundings enable listeners to synthesize the musical stream in concatenationist manner more effec-

12. For more on the nature of performative interpretation of musical compositions, see my "Performative versus Critical Interpretation in Music."

tively. But it will remain true that conscious attention on the listener's part to large-scale form, however much such form figures at the level of unconsious processing, is unnecessary for comprehending and rewarding musical experience.

Finally, the applicability of common critical descriptions of pieces or performances as "well paced," "broadly conceived," "carefully balanced," and so on—all apparently accolades presupposing appreciative grasp of overall form—can mostly be explained, I suspect, by reference to phenomenological properties of parts sequentially experienced, as opposed to properties revealed only in imaginative or intellectual contemplation of entire pieces or performances.

. . .

The central appreciative moral of concatenationism, one unaffected by the qualifications to the view that we have been brought to acknowledge, can be simply stated. In order to basically understand a piece of tonal instrumental music, or perhaps any music of teleological character, it is unnecessary to possess any explicit knowledge of the piece's formal structure or to maintain any awareness of its large-scale form. The only thing absolutely requisite is listening itself, grounded in sufficient prior exposure to related music and iterated sufficiently for the specific texture and movement of the given piece to be followed and responded to in its full individuality.[13]

Once that condition is achieved in regard to a given piece, three things may be said to ensure. First, the piece offers up to a listener most of the musical pleasure it is capable of providing. Second, the piece's basic expressiveness, and so the basis of any further expressiveness it may possess, becomes available to the listener. Third, the main part of a piece's value as music is made accessible to the listener, who is then in a position to gauge that value to a first approximation.

Qualified concatenationism[14] stands plain as a defense of the intuitive listener, assuming he or she is sufficiently dedicated to acquire the appro-

13. Note that this moral, which represents concatenationist listening as adequate for access to most of what is most worthwhile about instrumental music, is based not merely on observing how we do in fact listen to such music, but on noting what sort of listening capacity it is that is sufficient to yield an experience of a piece of music we are intuitively prepared to count as quite substantial appreciation of it.
14. I here allude to the caveats acknowledged in my summing up at the end of chapter 8.

priate listening background, and takes to heart the gentle commandment of adequate rehearsals. Concatenationism is intended, in particular, as a defense of such a listener against purveyors of intellectual appreciation of music primarily in terms of theoretical concepts, formal schemes, and spatial diagrams, and as a prophylactic or restorative against the fear or guilt occasioned by such approaches to appreciation.

The temple of serious music has its depths and heights, to be sure, and to penetrate certain of them, analytic insight or architectonic vision may be required. But a good part of the premises, and arguably their most important part, is open to all. One need only position oneself, through familiarity, in the right musicohistorical space, and then be willing to listen closely and repeatedly, until the unique shape of a given musical entity engraves itself on the mind's ear.

Understanding music, as we know, is at root being able to hear it in a certain way or experience it in a certain manner, and the long and short of it is that this ability can be achieved through repeated present-focused listening alone. The odd fact is that with music, acquaintance, if adequately backgrounded, extended, and deep, inevitably issues in comprehension of a fundamental sort: *connaître* becomes *savoir,* or perhaps *savoir faire.*

It is dispiriting to think of the many persons fully capable of appreciating the glories of classical music, to speak of no other kind—such as jazz— who have turned away without even venturing to cross the threshold, disheartened by the mistaken belief, which music theorists and commentators often do little to dispel, when they are not actively promoting it, that elaborate apprehensions of the form and technique of music are necessary to understanding it, and thus to reaping its proper rewards.[15] But the plain truth is that to appreciate any music of substance, the thing to do is listen to it, over and over again. That is the main prescription. Of course to experience the content of the music correctly, to respond to a piece as the piece it musicohistorically is, one must also have listened to and digested a lot of other music, in particular, that which forms the generative background to the piece in question. Still, *listening* is the

---

15. Compare Cook, once again, in *Music, Imagination, and Culture:* "The 'appreciation-racket' does not simply involve the idea that musical listeners should formulate representations of what they hear, it assumes that they should do so consciously" (p. 164).

key, internalizing a piece while implicitly situating it in the appropriate musicohistorical nexus, so that the piece's specific musical features have their proper, contextually grounded effects.[16] Contemplation of formal patterns, apprehension of spatial wholes, intellectual grasp of large-scale structural relations are of an entirely different, and lesser, order of importance. One can readily forgo them and still have entrée to the essential. Music for listening appreciation, of whatever scale or ambition, lives and dies in the moment—as no one has emphasized more effectively than Gurney—and it is there that it must be fundamentally understood, there that its fundamental value lies, whatever more rarefied excellences supervene on that foundation. No reflective analysis of or theoretical grip on musical architecture can substitute for the real-time synthetic apprehension of a musical work, part by part, in a chain of overlapping experiences of quasi-hearing, the fruit of attentive and informed listening. Nor, to underline the point once more, is the former in any way required for the latter.

16. For more on the contextual generation of the aesthetic and artistic contents of musical works, and the consequent requirements on listener preparation if those are to be rightly discerned, see my "What a Musical Work Is" and "Musical Literacy."

# WORKS CITED

Abraham, Gerald. *A Hundred Years of Music*. London: Duckworth, 1964.

Barford, Philip. *Bruckner Symphonies*. London: BBC Publication, 1978.

Beardsley, Monroe. *Aesthetics: Problems in the Philosophy of Criticism*. 1958; Indianapolis: Hackett, 1981.

Berg, Alban. "Why Is Schoenberg's Music So Difficult to Understand?" In *The Life and Work of Alban Berg,* ed. Willi Reich. London: Thames & Hudson, 1965.

Bonds, Mark Evan. *Wordless Rhetoric*. Cambridge: Harvard University Press, 1991.

Brettell, Richard, et al., eds. *The Art of Paul Gauguin*. Washington, D.C. National Gallery of Art, 1988.

Budd, Malcolm. *Music and the Emotions*. London: Routledge & Kegan Paul, 1985.

———. "Understanding Music." *Proceedings of the Aristotelian Society* 59, supplement (1985).

Clifton, Thomas. *Music as Heard*. New Haven: Yale University Press, 1983.

Cone, Edward. *Musical Form and Musical Performance*. New York: Norton, 1968.

———. "Three Ways of Reading a Detective Story—or, A Brahms Intermezzo." In *Music: A View from Delft*. Chicago: University of Chicago Press, 1989.

Cook, Nicholas. *Music, Imagination, and Culture*. New York: Oxford University Press, 1990.

——. "Musical Form and the Listener." *Journal of Aesthetics and Art Criticism* 46 (1987).

——. "The Perception of Large-Scale Tonal Closure." *Music Perception* 5 (1987).

Craig, Edward, ed. *The Routledge Encyclopedia of Philosophy*. London: Routledge, forthcoming.

Davies, J. B. *The Psychology of Music*. Stanford: Stanford University Press, 1979.

Davies, Stephen. "Attributing Significance to Unobvious Musical Relationships." *Journal of Music Theory* 27 (1983).

——. *Musical Meaning and Expression*. Ithaca: Cornell University Press, 1994.

DeBellis, Mark. *Music and Conceptualization*. Cambridge: Cambridge University Press, 1995.

Demuth, Norman. *Cesar Franck*. New York: Philosophical Library, 1949.

Gleitman, Henry. *Psychology*. 2d ed. New York: Norton, 1986.

Gurney, Edmund. *The Power of Sound* (1880). New York: Basic Books, 1966.

Hanslick, Eduard. *The Beautiful in Music* (1854). Trans. Gustav Cohen. Ed. Morris Weitz. Library of Liberal Arts, no. 45. New York: Liberal Arts Press, 1957.

Hindemith, Paul. *A Composer's World*. Cambridge: Harvard University Press, 1952.

Husserl, Edmund. *The Phenomenology of Internal Time-Consciousness*. Bloomington: Indiana University Press, 1964.

Karl, Gregory, and Jenefer Robinson. "Shostakovitch's Tenth Symphony and the Musical Expression of Cognitively Complex Emotions." *Journal of Aesthetics and Art Criticism* 53 (1995).

Kerman, Joseph. "Tovey's Beethoven." *American Scholar* 45 (1975).

Kivy, Peter. *Music Alone: Philosophical Reflections on the Purely Musical Experience*. Ithaca: Cornell University Press, 1990.

——. *Speaking of Art*. The Hague: Martinus Nijhoff, 1973.

Kramer, Lawrence. *Music as Cultural Practice, 1800–1900*. Berkeley: University of California Press, 1990.

Krausz, Michael, ed. *The Interpretation of Music: Philosophical Essays*. New York: Oxford University Press, 1993.

Kraut, Robert. "Perceiving the Music Correctly." In Krausz, *Interpretation of Music*.

Langer, Susanne. *Feeling and Form*. New York: Scribner's, 1953.

Levinson, Jerrold. "Evaluating Music." *Revue Internationale de Philosophie*, 198 (1996). Expanded version in *Musical Worlds: New Directions in the Philosophy of Music*, ed. Philip Alperson. University Park: Penn State University Press, forthcoming.

——. "Gurney, Edmund." In Craig, *Routledge Encyclopedia of Philosophy*.

——. "Hope in *The Hebrides*." In *Music, Art, and Metaphysics*.

——. *Music, Art, and Metaphysics: Essays in Philosophical Aesthetics.* Ithaca: Cornell University Press, 1990.

——. "Musical Expressiveness." In *Pleasures of Aesthetics.*

——. "Musical Literacy." In *Pleasures of Aesthetics.*

——. "Performative versus Critical Interpretation in Music." In *Pleasures of Aesthetics.*

——. *The Pleasures of Aesthetics: Philosophical Essays.* Ithaca: Cornell University Press, 1996.

——. "What a Musical Work Is." In *Music, Art, and Metaphysics.*

——. "What a Musical Work Is, Again." In *Music, Art, and Metaphysics.*

——. "What Is Aesthetic Pleasure?" in *Pleasures of Aesthetics.*

Lewis, C. I. *Analysis of Knowledge and Valuation.* La Salle, Ill.: Open Court, 1946.

Maus, Fred. "Music as Drama." *Music Theory Spectrum* 10 (1988).

McAdoo, Nick. "Hearing Musical Works in Their Entirety." *British Journal of Aesthetics* 37 (1997).

Meyer, Leonard. *Emotion and Meaning in Music.* Chicago: University of Chicago Press, 1956.

——. *Explaining Music.* Berkeley: University of California Press, 1973.

——. *Music, the Arts, and Ideas.* Chicago: University of Chicago Press, 1967.

Moore, G. E. *Principia Ethica* (1903). Cambridge: Cambridge University Press, 1959.

Newcomb, Anthony. "Narrative Archetypes and Mahler's Ninth Symphony." in *Music and Text: Critical Inquiries,* ed. Steven Paul Sher. New York: Cambridge University Press, 1992.

——. "Schumann and Late Eighteenth-Century Narrative Strategies," *19th-Century Music* 11 (1987): 164–174.

Newman, William. "Musical Form as a Generative Process." *Journal of Aesthetics and Art Criticism* 13 (1964).

Radcliffe, Philip. *Schubert Piano Sonatas.* London: BBC Publications, 1967.

Ridley, Aaron. *Music, Value, and the Passions.* Ithaca: Cornell University Press, 1995.

Riemann, Hugo. *Analysis of J. S. Bach's Preludes and Fugues, Part II.* London: Augener, 1893.

Sartre, Jean-Paul. *L'Imaginaire.* Paris: Gallimard, 1948.

Scruton, Roger. *The Aesthetic Understanding: Essays in the Philosophy of Art and Culture.* London: Methuen, 1983.

——. "Analytical Philosophy and the Meaning of Music." *Journal of Aesthetics and Art Criticism* 46 (1987).

——. *Art and Imagination: A Study in the Philosophy of Mind.* London: Methuen, 1974.

——. "Notes on the Meaning of Music." In Krausz, *Interpretation of Music.*

———. "Understanding Music." In *Aesthetic Understanding*.

Sessions, Roger. *The Musical Experience of Composer, Performer, Listener.* Princeton: Princeton University Press, 1950.

Sharpe, R. A. "Two Forms of Unity in Music." *Music Review* 44 (1983).

Sibley, Frank. "Making Music Our Own." In Krausz, *Interpretation of Music*.

Sloboda, John A. *The Musical Mind: The Cognitive Psychology of Music.* New York: Oxford University Press, 1985.

Storr, Anthony. *Music and the Mind.* New York: Free Press, 1992.

Tanner, Michael. "Understanding Music." *Proceedings of the Aristotelian Society* 59, supplement (1985).

Toch, Ernst. *The Shaping Forces in Music.* New York: Dover, 1977.

Tovey, Donald Francis. *A Companion to Beethoven's Pianoforte Sonatas.* London: Royal Schools of Music, 1931.

———. *Essays in Musical Analysis.* Vol. 1. London: Oxford University Press, 1935.

Wollheim, Richard. *The Thread of Life.* Cambridge: Harvard University Press, 1984.

Zuckerkandl, Victor. *Sound and Symbol: Music and the External World.* Trans. Willard R. Trask. New York: Pantheon, 1956.

# INDEX

**DATE DUE**